The Maxims of Robert E. Lee for Young Gentlemen

Advice, Admonitions, and Anecdotes on Christian Duty and Wisdom from the Life of General Lee

Compiled and edited by Richard G. Williams, Jr.
Foreword by John J. Dwyer

Best Wishes
Richard Williams

PELICAN PUBLISHING COMPANY
GRETNA 2006

Copyright © 2002, 2005
By Richard G. Williams, Jr.
All rights reserved

First edition, 2002
First Pelican edition, 2005
Second printing, 2006

*The word "Pelican" and the depiction of a pelican are trademarks
of Pelican Publishing Company, Inc., and are registered in the
U.S. Patent and Trademark Office.*

ISBN 9781589803107

All Scripture quotations are taken from the King James Version of the Bible.

*The photographs pertaining to Lee Chapel and Washington and Lee
University are used by permission of Lee Chapel and Washington and Lee
University in Lexington, Virginia.*

The photograph of the title page of Our Children in Heaven *was taken
from a copy in the author's library.*

Printed in the United States of America
Published by Pelican Publishing Company, Inc.
1000 Burmaster Street, Gretna, Louisiana 70053

To the Sons of Old Virginia,

"...in which we may also hear the echo of the voices of the statesmen, the soldiers and sages of bygone days, who have borne your name, and whose blood now flows in your veins."*

———

"The eyes of your countrymen are turned upon you, and again do wives and sisters, fathers and mothers and helpless children, lean for defense on your strong arms and brave hearts."

~ From Lee's General Order No. 16.

* These are the words of Julin Janney, President of the Virginia Secession Convention, welcoming Lee into the old House of Delegates chamber at the Capitol in Richmond on 25 April 1861.

Contents

Acknowledgments

W riting or editing a book, even one as humble as this one, requires the help of others. Without the work and dedication of previous authors and historians, this book would have been impossible. The book would also have been impossible were it not for the help and encouragement of my dear wife, Diane. Her patience as I spent hours upon hours in my basement office pecking on my keyboard and thumbing through stacks of books will earn her a crown. My daughters Mollie, Josie, and Olivia also suffered through an absent-in-mind, if not absent-in-body, father and I love them for that.

The image of Robert E. Lee with his three sons used for our cover design is from a painting by artist Janet McGrath, of Janet McGrath Studio (www.mcgrathstudio.com). This handsome depiction of Lee and his "young gentlemen" (*left to right: George Washington Custis Lee, William Henry Fitzhugh Lee, and Robert E. Lee, Jr.*)[1] was most fitting for our cover design and I am very grateful for Janet's kindness and generosity. I am honored to have this noble print grace a wall in the parlor of my home.

My fellow student of Lee, John J. Dwyer, an accomplished writer and scholar in his own right, did me a wonderful favor in agreeing to write the foreword to this second edition of *Maxims*. His two historical novels, *Stonewall* and *Robert E. Lee,* are great reads and worthy of additional consideration by students of Lee and Jackson. Another student of Lee, and one who is every bit the polished gentleman, Harry W. Crocker III, executive editor at Regnery Publishing, offered kind words of praise and encouragement as well. Harry's book, *Robert E. Lee on Leadership,* should be in every gentleman's library.

And I would certainly be remiss if I failed to mention and thank my late father, Guy Williams, for introducing me to General Lee when I was a young boy. He expressed his admiration for Lee when, in 1942, at just twelve years of age, he drew the pencil sketch of the good general shown on page 69. The sketch retains a place of honor on my office wall, reminding me daily of Lee's example and of my father's desire to share Lee's greatness with me. Oh that General Lee would again hold a place of honor in the hearts of young men as he once did. Perhaps, if God would be so gracious, this little book will in some small way contribute to a resurgence of young men's desire to emulate Robert E. Lee.

Finally, and of course, the most thanksgiving goes to my gracious God. Were it not for His loving and guiding Spirit and the sacrifice of His Son, I would likely be wifeless, childless, bookless, graceless, and worthless.

[1] General Lee often referred to Custis as "Boo" and to Fitzhugh as "Rooney."

Introduction

After Robert E. Lee had become President of what was then Washington College in Lexington, Virginia, he received a letter from an English nobleman offering him an annual salary of $50,000 to serve as president of a New York company promoting Southern commerce. This sum was over thirty times the $1500 Lee originally received as a college president. Characteristic of Lee's ever-present spirit of self-denial and sense of duty, he replied:

"I cannot leave my present position. I have a self-imposed task. I have led the young men of the South in battle. I must teach their sons to discharge their duty in life."

Lee's exemplary life still serves as an example to teach America's sons "to discharge their duty in life." Lee's life was the epitome of self-denial. His own selflessness when rejecting the offer of the command of the Federal forces at the outbreak of the War Between the States is perhaps one of the most striking examples of self-denial in human history. Lee walked away from almost certain victory and glory, and humbly accepted almost certain defeat and disgrace—all for duty's sake.

His struggle with that decision was not an easy one. Temperance, self-control, and self-denial—all of these attributes are defining characteristics of Lee and all central themes to the Christian faith. And all are character traits desperately needed by young men today. So it is that this little book is sent forth.

Contained in Lee's words is wisdom—wisdom sorely needed by the young men of our generation. Yet Lee's example is more than mere words. He was self-conscious of his duty, *manifested by his deeds,* and always concerned with the influence he might have upon others.

Lee once related an incident in which he was walking in the snow at Arlington. Lee's oldest son, Custis, was with him and he noticed that the boy was lagging behind. As Lee turned to look for his son, he noticed the young boy was carefully stepping in his father's deep footprints in the snow. In later telling of the incident, Lee said, "When I saw this, I said to myself, 'It behooves me to walk very straight, when this fellow is already following in my tracks.'"[1]

The quotes and anecdotes contained herein were collected and compiled over a number of years from various sources. The quotes come primarily from letters General Lee wrote to his children, his wife, soldiers, students, and acquaintances.

After General Lee's death, Baptist minister and Confederate Chaplain, J. William Jones discovered a worn military satchel among the General's personal belongings. In this satchel were found a number of sayings or personal "maxims" scribbled on pieces of paper. Jones referred to these as, "a great many maxims, proverbs, quotations from the Psalms, selections from standard authors, and reflections of his own."[2] Many of these had been written by Lee during the war and kept with him for years. According to one biographer, these were Lee's, "...moral pronouncements: preachments and moral stories for public use as well as personal benefit."[3] These maxims bear a strong resemblance to the advice directed to young men and contained in the verses in the Book of Proverbs, what the Scriptures call, "dark sayings." I refer to some of these as "Lee's Personal Maxims." Though not divinely inspired, they can, nonetheless, help point the way to wisdom and godliness.

Although not all of the quotes contained in this book were directed to "young gentlemen," it is to this class of American citizens that this modest volume is directed. General Lee once told someone, "Our country needs her young men now." That statement was no truer in Lee's day than it is in ours. I believe each maxim quoted, each admonition given, and each anecdote recounted, will give direction and guidance to young men as they strive for the lofty goal of becoming a Christian gentleman.

And as they strive, young men will do well to follow in Lee's footsteps, for *Robert E. Lee walked very straight.*

Pro Aris et Focis
Richard G. Williams, Jr.,
Thanksgiving 2004
Huckleberry Hollow, Virginia

[1] Rev. J. William Jones, D.D. *Life and Letters of Robert Edward E. Lee—Soldier and Man.* Originally published in 1906. (Reprint) Sprinkle Publications, Harrisonburg, VA, 1986, 42.

[2] Rev. J. William Jones, D.D., *Personal Reminiscences of General Robert E. Lee.* (Reprint) Tom Doherty Associates, LLC, New York, 2003, 132.

[3] Bishop Robert R. Brown, *And One Was a Soldier—The Spiritual Pilgrimage of Robert E. Lee.* White Mane Books, Shippensburg, PA, 1998, 56.

Foreword
by John J. Dwyer

Robert E. Lee has been discipling young and old men for a long time. You won't learn much of that in the standard television documentary or the mainstream academic text. You will find it by examining General Lee's own life and words.

What about the young men entrusted to his leadership during the War Between the States? The sweeping religious revivals in the Confederate armies, particularly Lee's Army of Northern Virginia, comprise one of the great overlooked chapters of the war, and one of the preeminent spiritual awakenings in American history.

The rough surroundings of wartime military camp life traditionally prove spawning grounds for every conceivable vice man can imagine. But Lee's devout leadership spurred contrary developments in his army. He facilitated an atmosphere where Christian belief and practice flourished. What did that spiritual movement look like?

Well, many of the card decks you would see were tossed aside by repentant soldiers marching the trail to war—and often replaced by prayer books, pocket testaments, or catechisms. Gambling and profanity alike were uncommon in this fearsome army.

Not only was the partaking of alcoholic spirits frowned upon by many in the army, but when stores of enemy liquor were captured, they were poured out onto the ground or burned—and that by order of the commanding officers.

Unlike most any other military force of the day, women of ill repute were not welcome in the van that followed Lee's army. And if it became known a soldier of the South was being unfaithful to a wife or causing a wife's unfaithfulness with his own actions, he risked cashiering.

You would observe more than one of Lee's captains profess belief in Christ after one of the camp's soul-searching sermons. Many of those officers would then call his company together, and remind them that they had followed him into many hard-fought battles, as well as into sin, and that he now wished his men to follow him into the blessed service into which he had just enlisted.

Up ahead, on a hillside, you might hear the chorus of over 2,000 manly voices echoing off the surrounding hills as they sang General Lee's favorite hymn, "How Firm a Foundation," in an open-air amphitheater built by a Virginia brigade.

Through the months you would witness the sermons and teaching of some of the greatest preachers in the South. Their common message, despite denominational distinctives, was the proclamation of Christ and Him crucified.

Lee did not merely permit or even promote such efforts; he himself participated with his whole heart. "General Lee used frequently to attend preaching at Jackson's headquarters," Lee's chaplain Dr. J. William Jones famously wrote, "and it was a scene which a master hand might have delighted to paint—those two great warriors, surrounded by hundreds of their officers and men, bowed in humble worship before the God and Saviour in whom they trusted."

You might even overhear Chaplain Jones tell Lee of the many fervent prayers offered on his behalf and the latter, renowned the length of the world for his military deeds, responding in a choked voice, "Please thank them for that, sir . . . And I can only say that I am nothing but a poor sinner trusting in Christ alone for my salvation, and need all of the prayers they can offer for me."

Perhaps only Oliver Cromwell and his Puritan army of "Roundheads" even approached the degree of orthodox devoutness of Robert E. Lee's army of young and not-so-young men.

Even more overlooked by the supposed experts and scholars are Lee's contributions during his final years of earthly life. Please understand, young man, that in the courts of true history, Providential history, Lee's greatest legacy is as a peacemaker, not a warrior. Following the war, the South lay in rubble, its manhood decimated, a harsh Federal military occupation further crushing it, and financial opportunists descending upon it from across the United States. Many Northerners desired the utter destruction of the South as a recognizable culture. Bitterness and hatred filled most former Confederates.

Lee recognized the issue was no less than the survival of the Southern people and their civilization. Wisdom formed his thoughts and actions. He rebuked younger officers who advocated continuing the war with guerrilla tactics; he refused to countenance or support large-scale emigration of Confederates to foreign lands; he urged Southerners to work lawfully and cheerfully within the existing laws of the United States to rebuild their fortunes and their land; and most of all, he beseeched them to forgive and forget wrongs committed against them by Federals past and present.

Business and financial opportunities cascaded in from around the world. But, as often he did, with his simple dignity and guileless ways, Lee surprised nearly everyone. He took the helm of tiny, war-ravaged Washington College in the backwater Virginia mountain village of Lexington, where Stonewall Jackson spent the decade before the war. With no assistant, scant budget, and beset by the burgeoning health problems of his aging body, he set about rebuilding the school, placing special emphasis on what curricula would best prepare the young men of the South to rebuild their land.

Yet many times, in many ways, he voiced his primary concern. Rev. Dr. James L. Kirkpatrick, professor of moral philosophy at Washington College, recalled Lee's words: "Oh, Doctor! If I could only know that all the young men in this college were good Christians, I should have nothing more to desire!"

Time and again he counseled forbearance and forgiveness on the part of his students, friends, family, and people across the South during the villainy of "Reconstruction": "The gentleman does not needlessly and unnecessarily remind an offender of a wrong he may have committed against him . . . He can not only forgive, he can forget; and he strives for that nobleness of self and mildness of character which imparts sufficient strength to let the past be but the past. A true man of honor feels humbled himself when he cannot help humbling others."

I used to think how much more eloquent I would have been than Lee had the mother asked me what advice she should give her baby when he grew older. Lee said simply, "Teach him he must deny himself." Having now lived a long time without Christ, and a long time with Him, I am beginning to understand Lee's simple, but profound wisdom. We are sinners and we want the wrong things, do we not? The life of Robert E. Lee teaches us that denying ourselves and preferring Christ is the hard but sure path both to earthly virtue and meaning, and eternal bliss and happiness.

And for those of us young—and not-so-young—men who

have slipped from that path or never entered upon it, it is not too late for any of us. Just keep right on reading to the next page and let Robert E. Lee disciple you, too.

John J. Dwyer is the author of the historical novels *Stonewall* and *Robert E. Lee,* and the historical narrative *The War Between the States, America's Uncivil War.* He serves as history chair at Coram Deo Academy, near Flower Mound, Texas.

Lee's Definition of a Gentleman

———⊷———

"The forebearing use of power does not only form a touchstone, but the manner in which an individual enjoys certain advantages over others is a test of a true gentleman. The power which the strong have over the weak, the magistrate over the citizen, and employer over the employed, the educated over the unlettered, the experienced over the confiding, even the clever over the silly—the forbearing or inoffensive use of all this power or authority, or a total abstinence from it when the case admits it, will show the gentleman in a plain light. The gentleman does not needlessly and unnecessarily remind an offender of a wrong he may have committed against him. He cannot only forgive, he can forget; and he strives for that nobleness of self and mildness of character which impart sufficient strength to let the past be but the past. A true man of honor feels humbled himself when he cannot help humbling others."

~ From Lee's own handwriting
found in Lee's worn military
satchel after his death by
Rev. J. William Jones.

CHAPTER 1

Humility

———◆·◆———

"The fear of the LORD is the instruction of wisdom;
and before honour is humility."

Proverbs 15:33

"Lee's lack of pride was his most endearing asset.
He took everyone seriously except himself."

Bishop Robert R. Brown

"In a few words, he cares but little for appearances,
though one of the handsomest men in the Confederacy,
and is content to take the same fare his soldiers get."

Peter W. Alexander

General Lee was never known to lash out in anger when reminded of the bitter defeat that he had suffered as Commander of the Confederate forces. The following exchange reveals Lee's humility and refusal to let even the most callous reminders provoke him:

"Perhaps there was never a better example of meekness under trying circumstances than the simple story of a sophomore who had been called before the president to be impressed with the fact that he must mend his ways or become a failure in life.

'But General, you *failed!*' answered the youth (who, no doubt, regretted that thoughtless remark all through his after life). The great man of his day and generation answered without the least resentment: 'I hope that you may be more fortunate than I.' "[1]

This battlefield encounter, recounted by a Union soldier at Gettysburg, is most touching and illustrative of Lee's Christian grace and humility, even in the midst of great bloodshed, affliction, and high emotion:

"I had been a most bitter anti-South man, and fought and cursed the Confederates desperately, I could see nothing good in any of them. A ball shattered my left leg. I lay on the ground not far from Cemetery Ridge, and as General Lee ordered his retreat, he and his officers rode near me. As they came along I recognized him, and, though faint from exposure and loss of blood, I raised up my hands, looked Lee in the face, and shouted as loud as I could—'Hurrah for the Union.' The General heard me, looked, stopped his horse, dismounted and came toward me. I must confess I at first thought he meant to kill me. But as he came up he looked down at me with such a sad expression upon his face that all fear left me, and I wondered what he was about. He extended his hand to me, grasping mine firmly, and looking right into my eyes, said: 'My son, I hope you will soon be well.' If I live to a thousand years I shall never forget the expression on General Lee's face. There he was defeated, retiring from a field that had cost him and his cause almost their last hope, and yet he stopped to say words like those to a wounded soldier of the opposition who had taunted him as he passed by! As soon as the General had left me, I cried myself to sleep there upon the bloody ground."[2]

"No man can be so important in the world that he need not the good-will and approval of others." ~ *One of Lee's personal maxims which he had the habit of scribbling on small slips of paper.*[3]

———

"Fame which does not result from good actions and achievements for the good of the whole people is not to be desired." ~ *One of Lee's personal maxims.*

———

"God is our only refuge and our strength. Let us humble ourselves before Him." ~ *From Lee's orders after Gettysburg, 21 August 1863.*

———

"In the good providence of God apparent failure often proves a blessing." ~ *Lee in a letter to George W. Jones, 22 March 1869.*

———

"You see what a poor sinner I am, and how unworthy to possess what was given me: for that reason it has been taken away." ~ *Lee to one of his daughters, 25 December 1861.*

———

"I am alone to blame . . . a younger and more abler man than myself can readily be obtained." ~ *Lee to Jefferson Davis after Gettysburg, 8 August 1864.*

———

"O, that I were more worthy and more thankful for all that He has done and continues to do for me!" ~ *Lee to his wife, 22 December 1861.*

———

"It is necessary we should be humble and taught to be less boastful, less selfish, and more devoted to right and justice to all the world." ~ *Lee to his wife, 8 February 1862.*

"If our people would only cease from vain self-boasting and adulation, how strong would be my belief in final success and happiness to our country." ~ *Lee to his wife, Christmas 1862.*

"There are but few who desire to read a true history of themselves." ~ *General Lee in a letter to Edward A. Palmer, 26 September 1866.*

"I do not care for display. The rank of Colonel is about as high as I ought ever to have gotten." ~ *General Lee's response when asked why he did not wear the full insignia of his rank.*

"I have a great reluctance to appear before the public in any manner. I think no good would result from it." ~ *General Lee in a letter to a Petersburg, Virginia lady, 21 May 1867.*

"I notice...that my mistakes are never told me until it is too late." ~ *General Lee after Gettysburg, 1863.*

"I know I fall far short of my obligations." ~ *Lee to his wife on the mercies of God, 25 April 1847.*

"My services have been performed alone in my tent, I hope with a humble, grateful and penitent heart, and will be acceptable to our Heavenly Father. May He continue His mercies to us both and all our children, relatives and friends, and in His own good time unite us in His worship, if not on earth, forever in Heaven." ~ *Lee to his wife, 12 April 1857.*

"I...feel more humbled by the praise of my friends (knowing how little I merit it) than the censure of my enemies." ~ *General Lee to the Honorable James M. Mason, 3 March 1870.*

"It matters little what they may do to me. I am old and have but a short time to live anyhow." ~ *Lee's reaction to being indicted for treason and rebellion.*

"I endeavored to give thanks to our Heavenly Father for all His mercies to me, for his preservation of me through all the dangers I have passed, and all the blessings he has bestowed upon me, for I know I fell far short of my obligations." ~ *Lee to son Custis from the battlefield in Mexico.*

"I find it so hard to try to keep one poor sinner's heart in the right way, that it seems presumptuous to try to help others." ~ *Lee to a friend on the duty to help others.*

"I hope my friends will give themselves no annoyance on my account, or any concern about the distribution of favors." ~ *Lee's thoughts on his own promotion during the Mexican War.*

"I am looking for some little quiet house in the woods

where I can procure shelter and my daily bread, if permitted by the victor." ~ *Lee to General Long after Appomattox.*

———

"I know of nothing good I could tell you of myself." ~ *Lee's response to a requested interview for a biography.*

———

"Reverses were necessary to make us brace ourselves for the work before us." ~ *Lee to one of his daughters, 26 February 1862.*

———

"I tremble for our country when I hear of confidence expressed in me. I know too well my weakness, and that our only hope is in God." ~ *Lee in a letter to his wife in 1863.*

———

"I believe it would be better in the end for us to suffer, keep right in our own eyes, the eyes of the world, and the eyes of God, and that justice would thereby be sooner done us." ~ *Lee to his son Custis, 7 August 1863.*

———

"I cannot even accomplish what I myself desire. How can I fulfill the expectations of others?" ~ *Lee to Jefferson Davis, 8 August 1863.*

———

"Life is indeed gliding away, and I have nothing good to show for mine that is past. I pray I may be spared to accomplish something for the benefit of mankind and the honor of God." ~ *Lee in a letter after accepting the presidency of Washington College.*

———•———

"The lower in position, the more suited to my ability and the more agreeable to my feelings." ~ *Lee to Jefferson Davis after Gettysburg.*

———•———

"I would have much preferred your choice had fallen upon an abler man." ~ *Lee upon accepting the Command of the Virginia forces.*

———•———

"I have enough and am content." ~ *Lee's response to once being offered a gift after the war.*

———•———

"Death in its silent, sure march is fast gathering those whom I have longest loved, so that when he shall knock at my door, I will more willingly follow." ~ *General Lee in 1869, just one year before his death.*

———•———

"I have no complaints to make of any one but myself." ~ *Lee to Jefferson Davis.*

———•———

"It's all my fault." ~ *Lee at Gettysburg.*

———•———

One final and well-documented incident of Lee's humility is worth mentioning. On a hot Sunday in June just after his surrender, General Lee was attending a communion service at St. Paul's Church in Richmond—the same church at which Confederate President Jefferson Davis had worshipped. Reverend Dr. Charles Minnegerode was at that time rector and invited those present to come forward to receive communion. The first to stand was a tall, neatly dressed black man. He walked to the front of the church and kneeled at the communion rail.

One who was in attendance later commented, "Its effect upon the communicants was startling, and for several moments they retained their seats in solemn silence and did not move, being deeply chagrined at this attempt to inaugurate the 'new regime' to offend and humiliate them...Dr. Minnegerode was evidently embarrassed."[4]

As the spirit of the astonished and agitated congregation grew tenser with each passing moment, another tall figure rose and made his way toward the altar. It was none other than Robert E. Lee. Lee calmly knelt next to his black brother and restored ease and grace to the rebuked assembly. Those gathered followed Lee's example and walked slowly forward; no doubt chastened by Lee's silent, but powerful example of reconciliation.

[1] Wayne Whipple, *The Heart of Lee.* The John C. Winston Co., Philadelphia, 1923, 217.

[2] Whipple, 171.

[3] A.L. Long, *Memoirs of Robert E. Lee—His Military and Personal History.* Originally published in 1886. (Reprint) The Blue and Grey Press, Secaucus, N.J., 1983, 485.

[4] Emory M. Thomas, *Robert E. Lee—A Biography.* W. W. Norton & Company, New York, 1995, 372.

CHAPTER 2

Education

"I have a self-imposed task. I have led the young men of the South in battle. I must teach their sons to discharge their duties in life."

R.E. Lee

"To give subtilty to the simple, to the young man knowledge and discretion."

Proverbs 1:4

"Our great want is a revival that shall bring these young men to Christ."

R.E. Lee

Someone once observed a visibly moved General Lee leaving a chapel service while serving as President of Washington College. When the observer inquired of Lee if something was wrong, Lee replied, "I was thinking of my responsibility to Almighty God for these hundreds of young men."

Robert E. Lee knew that education was more than the simple acquisition of knowledge. The following incident aptly illustrates Lee's understanding of true wisdom and education as revealed in Proverbs 9:10 ~ "The fear of the

LORD is the beginning of wisdom: and the knowledge of the holy is understanding."

———◆———

"Rev. Dr. Kirkpatrick, professor of moral philosophy in Washington College, relates the following concerning a conversation he had with General Lee just a short time previous to his fatal illness: 'We had been conversing for some time respecting the religious welfare of the students. General Lee's feelings soon became so intense that for a time his utterance was choked; but, recovering himself, with his eyes overflowed with tears, his lips quivering with emotion and both hands raised, he exclaimed: 'Oh Doctor! If I could only know that all the young men in the college were good Christians, I should have nothing more to desire.' "[1]

———◆———

"Avoid all frivolous authors, such as novel writers, and all skeptical authors, whether religious, philosophical or moral." ~ *These were the words of General Lee's father, Henry Lee, to General Lee's older brother, Carter. General Lee took this admonition to heart and would pass it on to his own children.*

———◆———

"The education of a man or woman is never completed until they die." ~ *Lee's acknowledgment of man's finite understanding in a letter to son Custis, 5 December 1860. William Hazlitt expressed the same thought with these words: "I have more confidence in the dead than the living."*

———◆———

"The more you know, the more you find there is to know in this grand and beautiful world. It is only the ignorant who suppose themselves omniscient." ~ *General Lee to his daughter, Mildred, 10 September 1863.*

"Our hardest lesson is self-knowledge, and it is one perhaps that is never accomplished." ~ *Lee in a letter to son Custis, 5 December 1860.*

"We must look to the rising generation for the restoration of the Country." ~ *General Lee to Virginia Governor John Lectcher in August of 1865.*

"You cannot be a true man until you learn to obey." ~ *Lee's personal maxim to his students at Washington College.*

"It is particularly incumbent on those charged with the instruction of the young to set them an example of submission to authority." ~ *From General Lee's letter accepting the position of President of Washington College, 24 August 1865.*

"One of the best ways that I know of to induce students to attend chapel is to be sure that we attend ourselves." ~ *General Lee's wise rebuke to a Washington College professor.*

"Gain knowledge and virtue and learn your duty to God and your neighbor. That is the great object of life." ~ *General Lee to his daughter, Mildred, Christmas 1862.*

"The first business of education is to draw forth and put into habitual exercise the former dispositions, such as kindness, justice, and self-denial." ~ *General Lee as President of Washington College.*

"Study hard, be always a gentleman, live cleanly, and remember God." ~ *General Lee to the students at Washington College.*

"Education embraces the physical, moral, and intellectual instruction of a child from infancy to manhood." ~ *General Lee to J.B. Minor, 17 January 1867.*

"Every one should do all in his power to collect and disseminate the truth, in the hope that it may find a place in history, and descend to posterity." ~ *General Lee to General P.T. Beauregard, 3 October 1865.*

"I shall be disappointed, sir—I shall fail in the leading object that brought me here, unless these young men all become consistent Christians." ~ *General Lee to Stonewall Jackson's Pastor, Dr. William S. White.*

"No one ever becomes too old to study the precious truths of the Bible." ~ *General Lee to a five year old boy.*

"Never touch a novel. They print beauty more charming than nature, and describe happiness that never exists." ~ *Lee advising his wife on reading material for his sons.*

"I consider the proper education of our youth one of the most important objects now to be attained and one which the greatest benefits may be expected." ~ *General Lee as President of Washington College.*

"I pray God to watch over and direct our efforts in guarding our little son, that we may bring him up in the way he should go." ~ *Robert E. Lee to his wife.*

"I prefer the Bible to any other book. There is enough in that to satisfy the most ardent thirst for knowledge; to open the way to true wisdom; and to teach the only road to salvation and eternal happiness. It is not above human comprehension, and it is sufficient to satisfy all its desires." ~ *Lee to wife Mary's cousin, Martha, "Markie" Williams.*

"We must expect reverses, even defeats. They are sent to teach us wisdom and prudence, to call forth greater energies, and to prevent our falling into greater disasters." ~ *General Lee to Jefferson Davis, 5 August 1863.*

"Time and experience, the great teachers of men under the guidance of an ever-merciful God, may save us from destruction." ~ *General Lee to Captain M.F. Maury, 8 September 1865.*

"Let nothing discourage or deter you from endeavoring to acquire virtue and knowledge." ~ *Lee to his sons, 30 November 1845.*

"Learn to be good. Be true, kind, and generous and pray earnestly to God to enable you to keep His commandments, and walk in the same all the days of your life." ~ *Lee to his sons, 31 March 1846.*

31

[1] J. Williams Jones, D.D., *Christ in the Camp.* Originally published in 1887. (Reprint) Sprinkle Publications, Harrisonburg, VA, 1986, 78.

CHAPTER 3

Christian Faith

———◆◆◆———

"My chief concern is to try to be an humble, earnest Christian."

R.E. Lee

"The Christian character of General Lee was one in which the tenderness, forgiveness, philanthropy, and purity of the real disciple of the true Christ conception were the ruling impulses and not the haughty, austere self-satisfaction or the unrelenting exacting creed of those who consider themselves elect."

General A.L. Long

"He thought of each man in his army as a soul to be saved and in every way he could encouraged the mission and revival work . . . Even in the midst of urgent duty he would stop and take part in a camp prayer-meeting, and listen to the exhortations of some ragged veteran, as a young convert might listen to an apostle."

Gamaliel Bradford

Robert E. Lee's Christian faith is well known and documented in over two-thousand letters and correspondences that have, fortunately, been preserved. His exemplary life further testified of his walk with Christ and he was, in the words of Apostle Paul, ". . . our epistle written in our hearts, known and read of all men"—II Corinthians 3:2. General Lee had many friends who were members of the clergy, most notably—Bishop William Meade (His first teacher at Christ Church in Alexandria), Bishop John Johns of Virginia, General William Nelson Pendleton (Lee's Pastor in Lexington), Rev. William S. White (Stonewall Jackson's Pastor), Rev. J. William Jones (A Baptist Pastor and Confederate Chaplain), and many other Christian ministers who Lee looked to for spiritual leadership and Christian example. Each man made marked contributions to Lee's spiritual life.

Nonetheless, it is difficult to establish with certainty the exact time and place of Lee's conversion. Some have argued that it took place on July 17, 1853, when General Lee responded to the sermon "Lord, to whom shall we go?" preached in Christ Church in Alexandria by Bishop John Johns. At the close of the sermon General Lee went forward and knelt at the communion rail, along with two of his daughters, Mary and Anne. But it is likely that this was simply Lee's public confession of Christ, as a careful examination of his outward attitude, letters, and comments reveal he underwent a conspicuous change during the war with Mexico, somewhere between 1847 and 1848. The exposure to the bloody battlefield had left an unmistakable impression upon Lee as he noted in several letters. He was suddenly much more aware of the frailty and brevity of human life. One biographer noted the change:

"The certain fact is that during the Mexican War Lee began to write and speak with a pronounced conviction and warmth about a loving Father in Heaven who had guided and protected him and to whom he owed abundant gratitude...During this time a subtle, yet perceptible softening of personality was evident to many outside the family."[1]

This was not a "conversion of convenience" just to get Lee through the horrors of war. Though Lee had lived a religious and morally upright life since his childhood, henceforth his faith revealed a much more personal relationship with his Heavenly Father—and everyone noticed:

"The strict moral character and manifest talent his peers had always admired were infused now with a greater glow of affectionate outreach which changed their respect to devotion . . . Everybody and everything—his family, his friends, his horse, and his dog, loves Colonel Lee."[2] Robert E. Lee was a "new creature in Christ."[3] He had chosen the narrow path and his decision would prove to be a godly influence upon countless others who would also choose that same path.

———

"The Bible is the Book of Books." ~ *Lee's estimate of the Scriptures.*

———

"Above all things, learn at once to worship your Creator and to do His will as revealed in His Holy Book." ~ *General Lee's advice to a child who had been named after him.*

———

"God disposes. This ought to satisfy us." ~ *One of General Lee's personal maxims.*

———

"May God give you strength to bear the affliction He has imposed, and produce future joy out of your present misery, is my earnest prayer." ~ *General Lee to Daughter-in-law Charlotte, reflecting upon the death of her infant daughter.*

———

"As soon as I order them forward into battle, I leave my army in the hands of God." ~ *Lee on God's watch-care.*

"I can only say that I am a poor sinner, trusting in Christ alone, and that I need all the prayers you can offer for me." ~ *General Lee to Rev. Beverly Tucker Lacy.*

"The defenders of a just cause should be pure in His eyes." ~ *From Lee's General Order No. 63.*

"Be true, kind, and generous, and pray earnestly to God to enable you to keep His commandments and walk in the same all the days of your life." ~ *Lee to one of his sons, 31 March 1846.*

"Oh, that we may be at last united in that heaven of rest, where trouble and sorrow never enter, to join in an everlasting chorus of praise to our Lord and Savior." ~ *General Lee to his son Fitzhugh, when Fitzhugh's wife passed away.*

"It is satisfactory always to have facts to go on; they restrain supposition and conjecture, confirm faith, and bring contentment." ~ *Lee to his wife, 27 December 1856.*

"Let us humble ourselves before the Lord our God, asking through Christ, the forgiveness of our sins, beseeching the aid of the God of our forefathers in the defense of our homes and our liberties." ~ *From Lee's General Order No. 23.*

"Providence requires us to use the means He has put under our own control." ~ *Lee to his wife, 19 April 1857.*

"May God rescue us from the folly of our acts, save us from selfishness, and teach us to love our neighbors as ourselves." ~ *General Lee to his son, 30 January 1861.*

"I look forward to better days, and trust that time and experience, the great teachers of men, under the guidance of an ever-merciful God, may save us from destruction, and restore to us the bright hopes and prospects of the past." ~ *General Lee to Captain M.F. Maury, 8 September 1865.*

"I have fought against the people of the North because I believed they were seeking to wrest from the South dearest rights. But I have never cherished bitter or vindictive feelings, and have never seen the day when I did not pray for them." ~ *General Lee's feelings of charity towards his enemies after the war.*

"We cannot be always successful and reverses must come. May God give us courage, endurance, and faith to strive to the end." ~ *General Lee to his son Custis, 3 September 1861.*

"God will shield us and give us success." ~ *General Lee to his wife, 23 February 1862.*

"God knows what is best for us." ~ *General Lee to his wife, 9 July 1862.*

"Truth and justice will at last prevail." ~ *General Lee to one of his sons, 26 February 1867.*

"I believe a kind God has ordered all things for our good." ~ *General Lee to his wife, 4 December 1863.*

"The ties to earth are taken, one by one, by our Merciful God to turn our hearts to Him and to show us that the object of this life is to prepare for a better and brighter world." ~ *General Lee to his cousin Margaret Stuart, 29 December 1863.*

"My whole trust is in God, and I am ready for whatever He may ordain." ~ *General Lee to his son, Fitzhugh, 24 April 1864.*

"God does not always give the battle to the strong." ~ *General Lee to his wife, 21 February 1865.*

"Commanding officers will require the usual inspections on Sunday to be held at such time as not to interfere with the attendance of the men on divine service at the customary hour in the morning." ~ *From Lee's General Order No. 15, 7 February 1864.*

"I want all the husbands in the field, and their wives at home encouraging them, loving them, and praying for them." ~ *General Lee to son Fitzhugh's wife, Charlotte.*

"We must rely for guidance and protection upon a kind Providence." ~ *General Lee to his wife, 21 February 1865.*

"I salute the Church of God!" ~ *General Lee to a Confederate Chaplain.*

"Let us then oppose constancy to adversity, fortitude to suffering, and courage to danger, with the firm assurance that He who gave freedom to our fathers will bless the efforts of their children to preserve it." ~ *From Lee's General Order No. 2, 14 February 1865.*

"God provides for our pleasure in every way." ~ *General Lee to one of his daughters, 25 December 1861.*

"I feel confident that with the blessing of God what seems to be our greatest danger will prove the means of deliverance and safety." ~ *General Lee to Governor Vance of North Carolina, 24 February 1865.*

"With calm satisfaction, trust in God and leave results to Him." ~ *General Lee to Rev. J. William Jones.*

"We must all try to be good Christians—that is the most important thing." ~ *General Lee to a five year old boy.*

"No day should be lived unless it was begun with a prayer of thankfulness and an intercession for guidance." ~ *General Lee—The General was notoriously strict with his family about being on time for morning prayers—promptly at 7 AM.*

"I dread the thought of any student going away from the college without becoming a sincere Christian." ~ *General Lee to Dr. William White, Stonewall Jackson's Pastor.*

[1] Bishop Robert R. Brown, *And One Was a Soldier—The Spiritual Pilgrimage of Robert E. Lee.* White Mane Books, Shippensburg, PA, 1998, 25.

[2] Brown, 25.

[3] II Corinthians 5:17

CHAPTER 4

Duty

———◆———

"He hath shewed thee, O man, what is good; and what doth the LORD require of thee, but to do justly, and to love mercy, and to walk humbly with thy God?"

Micah 6:8

Chivalry ~ "...a romantic idealism closely related to Christianity, which makes honor the guiding principle of conduct. Connected with this is the ancient concept of the gentleman."

Richard Weaver

To know Lee, one must understand the depth of his deliberate commitment to the principle of duty. It guided every decision he made—often at great personal sacrifice. Nowhere was this commitment and sacrifice more obvious than in its influence on Lee in his decision to decline the Union's offer of Commander of all Union forces and to suffer the fate of his native Virginia. There could be no possible motive for glory or riches; for Lee was fully aware of the likely outcome of a struggle against the numerically superior North. He was also aware that, contrary to the opinion of many, it would be a long and bloody conflict. His only motive was—what is my duty and, as a Christian, what is the will of God? It was a question that Providence seemed to have dictated to not only Lee, but also to his forefathers—"...the voices of the statesmen, the soldiers and sages of bygone days, who have borne your name, and whose blood now flows in your veins."[1]

Those voices "of bygone days" would reach across centuries and continents and cry out to Lee while he was in the midst of the most consequential decision of his life. One of these voices called to Lee from a land north of the River Tweed, on the border with England—the unearthly and beautiful land of Scotland. A land inhabited by a hardy breed of Celts whose history is rich with romantic stories of chivalry, bravery, and heroic struggles for freedom—a land so full of legends and myths, it's sometimes difficult to separate true history from the romanticized version. It is said that Scotland and its history are sung more in ballad than any other place on earth. One thing is certain. For hundreds of years, the Scots fought many bloody and cruel wars with their neighbor to the South, England, in Scotland's struggle for independence. The love of liberty and freedom is always just below the skin of a Scot who knows his history. In recent years there has been a renewed interest about Scottish history, thanks in large measure to Mel Gibson's 1995 film, *Braveheart;* the inspiring story about Scottish warrior and hero, Sir William Wallace.

In 1306, another Scottish warrior, and contemporary of William Wallace, was involved in this epic struggle for Scotland's liberty. This warrior was not fighting for Scotland however, but for the English in opposition against his native land. Tradition has it that shortly after a particularly bloody battle, this man sat down to eat and celebrate the victory with his English comrades. Robert the Bruce was about to be faced with a decision that would alter the course of history and that of his cherished Scotland.

The torturous death of William Wallace, at the hands of King Edward of England for his rebellion against the throne, tormented the mind of Bruce, preventing him from enjoying the revelry of the victory. Try as he might, his conscience would not let him forget Wallace's courage and steadfastness—two traits that Wallace kept to the end. Traits he kept even as he was castrated and disemboweled alive, the final act of death accomplished by the King's executioner as he reached into Wallace's chest and tore out his still beating heart. This grotesque and cruel execution took place before a jeering, bloodthirsty mob of English peasants and nobles as one of Wallace's men held high his psalter. Prior to his execution, Wallace had made the request to hold the psalter up in plain view so he could gaze upon its pages, bringing forth distracting memories of happier times when he had serenaded his God with the Psalms of David as he roamed Scotland's green mountains and valleys. Robert had also watched as Wallace's head was impaled on a spike high on London Bridge and the four quarters of his body were taken to Newcastle, Berwick, Perth, and Stirling to be put on display, lest any other Scottish fool have some vain notion of "freedom." Yet, even in death, William Wallace bedeviled the British and entreated the Scots to fight for their homeland:

"As the flesh rotted away from the right arm and shoulder of the martyred hero, and the sun-dried sinews tightened, the skeletal hand of Wallace seemed to rise on the gibbet of Newcastle and point longingly to the north. Wallace had been denied the opportunity to die on his native soil...now, it seemed, his mortal remains were directing his spirit remains back to Scotland." [2]

This ghostly scene, along with the image of Wallace's bravery in the midst of a merciless execution, was forever etched into Bruce's mind and served as a constant reminder not only of William Wallace's devotion to Scotland's liberty, but of Bruce's own reputation as a traitor. The contrast cursed him. Bruce's decision to fight for the English had been a pragmatic one. Though Bruce had once fought with Wallace against the English, he became fearful after Scotland's defeat at Falkirk; fearful that Scotland's quest for freedom was hopeless and that any further struggle against the English Crown was futile and would cost him his vast estate, if not his life.

So Bruce bowed and submitted to Edward while his patriotic brethren continued their resistance toward the English Throne and Bruce raised his sword against his own kin. It was shortly after one of these battles in which Robert the Bruce fought alongside the English, assisting them as he slaughtered his fellow Scotsmen, that he sat with the English noblemen to break bread and celebrate their victory over the rebellious Scots.

Bruce had fought valiantly and proved his devotion to King Edward. He thought he deserved the respect of the English lords, if not of his own conscience. As Bruce sat down to eat, his unwashed hands still stained with the blood of his own countrymen, he noticed snickers among the English nobles. He overheard one of them whisper, "Look at that Scotsman, who is eating his own blood!"[3] The words pierced his heart like a hot dagger. He was simultaneously overwhelmed with anger and shame—his face first flushing with rage then becoming ashen with self-realization. He was a Judas. Robert the Bruce now had a decision to make. Would he accept the scorn and mockery he deserved and go down in history as a traitor to his native sod, or would he repent, risking his worldly wealth and position, embrace honor and cast his lot with his kinsmen and their uncertain future?

Across the Atlantic and some 555 years later, a descendant of Robert the Bruce[4] paces the floor in an upstairs room of his home. His home lay just South of the Potomac River in another land also steeped in legend and history with gallant tales of bravery, chivalry, and a passionate love of liberty. This Robert is faced with a very similar decision. Perhaps Robert E. Lee's soul was haunted by the memory of Bruce's experience as he prayerfully struggles with the most agonizing decision he will ever make. It's the night of April the nineteenth, 1861. Though Lee's humility prevented him from speaking publicly of his ancestry, he was well aware that he was "well descended." Perhaps his mother had recounted the shame of Bruce's conduct to young Robert as she filled the role of an absent father. No doubt he had read the story of Bruce's conflict and Scotland's valiant struggle for liberty. It is also very likely that the young Robert Lee was inspired by the heroic tales of Scotland's best known writer, Sir Walter Scott (1711-1832) and the medieval history of Scott's native land. Scott's influence on Southerners is well known—

"It was due to this universal love of adventure—this hunger for an active and stirring life,—that Sir Walter Scott enjoyed such extraordinary popularity in the homes of the Southern people. There were few libraries of importance among them that were lacking in those splendid volumes in which he has drawn such romantic pictures..." [5]

The struggle that Robert E. Lee was faced with was the same one that confronted Robert the Bruce. Their initial decisions and the ultimate consequences were, however, very different. After Fort Sumter, Lincoln had called upon the several states to provide seventy-five thousand militia for ninety days service to put down the "rebellion." Robert E. Lee's native land, Virginia, answered with a call for secession. The Old Dominion and cradle of liberty that had given birth to the likes of George Washington, Thomas Jefferson, and Patrick Henry would not stand for such heavy-handed oppression. Figuratively speaking, and in the collective memory of Virginians, her soil was still moist with the blood of the British and, if necessary, in the words of Jefferson, additional blood would be fitting:

"The tree of liberty must be refreshed from time to time with the blood of patriots and tyrants." [6]

Colonel Robert E. Lee, United States Army, would now make the decision that would alter the course of history—and that of his beloved Virginia.

Robert E. Lee had given his whole life to the Union for which his father, Henry Lee, the famous, "Lighthorse Harry Lee," had fought. Robert was born at the Lee ancestral mansion, Stratford Hall, and drew his first breath in the same room in which were born two signers of the Declaration of Independence, Richard Henry Lee and Francis Lightfoot Lee. He had married Mary Custis, the daughter of George Washington Parke Custis, who was the adopted grandson of George Washington. Lee's strong ties to the Union, and its founding, were both by blood and by choice. The depth of Lee's love for, and loyalty to, the Union is something many students of Lee fail to give due consideration. It makes his decision all the more remarkable. By the age of 54, Colonel Robert E. Lee had fought with honor and distinction in the Mexican War, served as Superintendent of West Point, quelled a domestic insurrection at Harper's Ferry, and was a highly respected officer and engineer. Lee's military prowess was well recognized. General Winfield Scott credited the United States' victory over Mexico to the "skill, valor and undaunted energy of

Robert E. Lee" and once referred to him as, "the greatest military genius in America." Lee and General Scott enjoyed mutual respect and admiration.

President Lincoln was no fool for offering the command of the Union forces to Lee. Not only was it the prevailing opinion that Lee was the most qualified to take command, Lincoln knew that if Lee accepted, his stature alone might bring a quicker end to the conflict. The offer would test Lee's loyalties and lead to the spiritual struggle of a lifetime. Lee's mind was already made up when it came to fighting against Virginia. He could not bring himself to raise his sword against his kinfolk and ancient homeland. On April the 18th, 1861, after declining Lincoln's offer, Lee went immediately to General Scott's office in Washington and informed him of his decision. Lee's friend and comrade in arms responded with a statement Lee had not fully anticipated:

"...I feared it would be so...If you purpose to resign, it is proper that you should do so at once; your present attitude is equivocal." [7]

Until now, Lee had remained hopeful he would not be forced to resign from the Army he loved unless and until Virginia seceded and her citizens affirmed the ordinance of secession. That hope was now dashed. Though Lee had declined the offer of command, he would not be able to deny service if he were called upon for duty once hostilities commenced. Scott had made that painfully clear. At that point, Lee would have to "...resign under orders. That was a disgrace to any soldier." [8]

In fact, Virginia did pass an ordinance of secession on the afternoon of April 17th, but had kept the news secret until Virginia militia units could seize Federal arsenals within its borders. Lee read the headlines two days later on the morning of April 19th. His heart sank. With great despair in his heart and a feeling of impending doom in the air, Lee rode home to Arlington. He would never again cross the Potomac as an officer in the United States Army. After supper at Arlington that same evening, Lee walked slowly up the stairs to his room knowing full well that he would be wrestling with his God and his devotion to the Union for hours. Lee was facing his Gethsemane. Downstairs, his wife Mary heard him drop to his knees in prayer, then up on his feet again to continue pacing back and forth as the momentous struggle wore on—Oh, how he wished this cup might pass! What of his career? What of the revered Union? What of his family's well-being? What of the future of his native Virginia, in whose soil slept the dust of his fathers?

No doubt Robert E. Lee thought more than once that night of his father. Light Horse Harry Lee was a favorite of General Washington and was chosen by Congress to eulogize our first president. It was in his eulogy of Washington that Lee's father first coined the phrase, "First in war, first in peace and first in the hearts of his countrymen." It is likely that these were not the only words of Lee's father that came to his mind as he struggled that spring evening. During a debate in 1798 with James Madison, Lee's father had stated, "Virginia is my country; her will I obey, however lamentable the fate to which it may subject me." Those words likely burned into his soul as the great warrior weighed his loyalties:[9]

"Reared in this school and under these influences, Robert Edward Lee regarded his allegiance to the sovereign State of Virginia as paramount to all other, and that he must obey her voice at whatever sacrifice of feeling, or of personal interest."[10]

The eminent Virginia historian, Philip Alexander Bruce, expressed this sentiment with these words:

"It was this love of home, with its thronging recollections of the past

both near and far . . . that nerved many a Southern soldier . . . Love of the South was inextricably mixed up with this love of the family hearth . . . Love of one particular spot, of one neighborhood, of one State, was the foundation stone of the love of the entire region which entered so deeply into the spirit of the Confederate soldier." [11]

The Lees were "Virginians of Virginians." How could he raise his sword against his native land and against his own kin? Mary Lee would later write of her husband's contest with self that historic night: "My husband has wept tears of blood over this terrible war." [12] Finally, after midnight, a spiritually drained Lee solemnly descended the stairs to the sitting room where Mary had waited and said, "Well Mary, the question is settled. Here is my letter of resignation and a letter I have written General Scott." [13] These were those letters:

Arlington, Washington City P.O., April 20, 1861.

Hon. Simon Cameron,
Secretary of War.

Sir:—I have the honor to tender the resignation of my commission as colonel of the First Regiment of Cavalry

Very respectfully,

Your obedient servant,
R.E. Lee

Arlington, Va., April 20, 1861.

General: -
Since my interview with you on the 18th inst., I have felt that I ought no longer to retain my commission in the Army. I therefore tender my resignation, which I request you will recommend for acceptance. It would have been presented at once but for the struggle it has cost me to separate myself from a service to which I have devoted all the best years of my life and all the ability I possessed.

49

During the whole of that time—and more than a quarter century,—I have experienced nothing but kindness from my superiors, and the most cordial friendship from my comrades. To no one, General, have I been as much indebted as to yourself for uniform kindness and consideration, and it has always been my ardent desire to meet your approbation. I shall carry to the grave the most grateful recollections of your kind consideration, and your name and fame will always be dear to me.

Save in the defense of my native State, I never desire again to draw my sword. Be pleased to accept my most earnest wishes for the continuance of your happiness and prosperity, and believe me,

Most truly yours,
R.E. Lee.

In the words of Douglas Southall Freeman, it was "the decision Lee was born to make."[14] The travail of prayer had rendered its fruit. Lee would cast his lot with Virginia, in full measure—there was no other thing he could do. Though he opposed secession and had termed it "revolution," he also would state, "A union that can only be maintained by swords and bayonets...has no charm for me."[15] Even after the war, as the South lay in ruin, Lee would affirm the rightness of his decision:

"I did only what my duty demanded. I could have taken no other course without dishonour. And if it all were to be done over again, I should act in precisely the same manner."[16]

Lee had done his duty and the personal sacrifice would be enormous. Our current age is guided by the antithesis of duty—selfishness. Whether it pertains to government officials or business executives, too often we hear the report of a selfish act motivated by the base desire of self-preservation or profit at the expense of one's duty. Young men who wish to lay claim to the noble title of "gentleman" must embrace their duty at all costs and in the face of sometimes-fierce opposition and personal loss.

This willingness to suffer loss and shame for doing what is right is what our Saviour spoke of in Matthew 16:24, when He said, "...If any man will come after me, let him deny himself, and take up his cross, and follow me." In deciding to resign from an illustrious career rather than violate principles he held dear, and which he consecrated in an earnest struggle with his God, Lee humbly took up his cross and denied himself. For Lee, it was the right thing to do.

Those familiar with Lee's legendary military successes while leading the Army of Northern Virginia need no further explanation of the consequences of Lee's decision. His glorious victories against overwhelming odds have inspired volumes. Though the South ultimately lost, the Confederacy's greatest general is as much recognizable as any in history, and more admired than any officer the North can claim. Lee became an unwilling Christ figure for Southerners—"Greater love hath no man than this, that a man lay down his life for his friends." ~ *John 15:13*

Lee would cringe at such an analogy and certainly no sacrilege is intended. Yet the comparison is undeniable and, if one believes the Bible and our command to be Christ-like, wholly appropriate. God knows we need some Christ-likeness to emulate in our day.

So what of Lee's progenitor, Robert the Bruce? Bruce was so sickened by his own traitorous conduct that he rose from the table, went immediately to a nearby chapel and fell upon the altar. There he wept bitter tears of repentance, praying for forgiveness and vowing to God to never again raise his hand against Scotland. Robert the Bruce kept his vow, ultimately freeing Scotland from the English yoke and becoming King of Scotland. Thus Bruce had achieved the dreams of William Wallace.

Though their paths and outcomes were different, both Robert E. Lee and Robert the Bruce are revered in their homelands today. Both men, through the intervention of Divine supplication, chose the path of duty, honor, and sacrifice and, in so doing, altered the course of history. Both died heroes bound by ancestry and by Providence. Perhaps it was Providence speaking and reminding humanity of these two warriors' ties as Robert E. Lee met the final enemy.

As Lee lay dying in Lexington, Virginia, the stormy October sky flashed with an unusual light for several nights in a row. According to Douglas Southall Freeman, "some saw in it a beckoning hand"[17] and a Lexington woman took from a bookshelf a copy of The Lays of the Scottish Cavaliers and pointed with eerie assurance to a passage from Aytoun's "Edinburgh after Flodden":

"All night long the northern streamers
Shot across the trembling sky:
Fearful lights, that never beckon
Save when kings or heroes die."

Though dead, both men still serve as examples of what adherence to duty may sometimes cost. Both men's lives point, as did William Wallace's decaying hand, to what most moderns don't understand—duty and God-inspired love of native-sod.

———◆·◆———

"Do your duty. That is all the pleasure, all the comfort, all the glory we can enjoy in this world." ~ *General Lee to his son Custis, 3 September 1861.*

———◆·◆———

"I am but doing my duty, and with me, in small matters as well as in large ones, duty must come before pleasure." ~ *Lee to General Magruder in Mexico.*

"Private and public life are subject to the same rules; and truth and manliness are two qualities that will carry you through this world much better than policy, or tact, or expediency, or any other word that was ever devised to conceal or mystify a deviation from a straight line." ~ *One of Lee's personal maxims.*

"Every student must be a gentleman." ~ *General Lee to a student and his one rule for all students at Washington College.*

"We must make up our minds to fight our battles ourselves, expect to receive aid from no one, and make every necessary sacrifice." ~ *General Lee to his son, Custis, 29 December 1861.*

"We have humbly tried to do our duty. We may, therefore, with calm satisfaction, trust in God, and leave results to Him." ~ *General Lee in a conversation with J. William Jones in 1866.*

"Let each heart grow strong in the remembrance of our glorious past." ~ *From Lee's General Order No. 16.*

"It is our duty to live, for what will become of the women and children of the South if we are not here to support and protect them?" ~ *General Lee just before the surrender at Appomattox.*

"Take with you the satisfaction that proceeds from the consciousness of duty faithfully performed." ~ *From General Lee's farewell address to his army.*

"Let every man remember that all he holds dear depends upon the faithful discharge of his duty." ~ *From Lee's General Order No. 102, 26 November 1863.*

"There is a true glory and a true honor: the glory of duty done—the honor of the integrity of principle." ~ *One of Lee's personal maxims.*

"Stand up...boldly, manfully; do your best." ~ *Lee to his son Custis, 28 December 1851.*

"We want to be true to ourselves, to be prudent, just, and bold." ~ *General Lee to his son, Custis, 29 December 1861.*

"Think always of your father." ~ *General Lee to one of his daughters, Christmas Day, 1861.*

"Try and do your best, and if that does not recompense you for your devotion and labor, you will find it in the happiness which it brings to father and mother." ~ *Lee to son Custis, 4 May 1851.*

———•———

"I cannot consent to desert my native state in the hour of her adversity, I must abide her fortunes and share her fate." ~ *General Lee's reply to an English nobleman upon his offer of a home in England.*

———•———

"The duties exacted of us by civilization and Christianity are not less obligatory in the country of the enemy than in our own." ~ *From Lee's General Orders No. 73, Chambersburg, PA, 27 June 1863.*

———•———

"It must be remembered that we make war only upon armed men." ~ *From Lee's General Orders No. 73.*

———•———

"You have a sacred charge, the care of your poor mother." ~ *General Lee to daughter Agnes, 25 May 1863.*

———•———

"We must make up our minds to meet with reverses and overcome them." ~ *General Lee to his wife, 8 February 1862.*

———•———

"You must do all you can for our dear country." ~ *General Lee to one of his daughters, 26 February 1862.*

———•———

"Men will most effectively secure their safety by preserving order and fighting with coolness and vigor." ~ *General Lee to his subordinates, 22 February 1865.*

———•———

"Discipline cannot be attained without constant watchfulness." ~ *General Lee to his subordinates, 22 February 1865.*

———•———

"All are urged to do nothing which may disturb the peace, harmony, and happiness that should pervade a Christian community." ~ *General Lee to his students at Washington College, Christmas Eve, 1869.*

———•———

"Abstinence form spirituous liquors is the best safeguard to morals and health." ~ *General Lee to the "Friends of Temperance" in Lexington, VA, 9 December 1869.*

———•———

General Lee was well aware of the dangers of alcohol and it's notoriety in destroying the character of young men. During the war, some of Lee's younger officers were known to enjoy a good drink and Lee wanted to make his disapproval known. After seeing a jug of strong drink brought to an officer's tent, Lee had a jug dispatched to his own tent. He then invited the young officers to share a drink of "the best." Due to Lee's known aversion for liquor, they were taken aback by the invitation. Nonetheless, they accepted but were chagrined when Lee filled their glasses with buttermilk![18]

———•———

"I cannot too earnestly exhort you to practice habitual temperance, so that you may form the habit in youth, and not feel the inclination, on temptation, to depart from it in manhood." ~ *General Lee to the "Friends of Temperance" in Lexington, VA, 9 December 1869.*

———•———

"Obedience to lawful authority is the foundation of manly character." ~ *General Lee's oft' repeated personal maxim to many.*

———————

"As a general principle you should not force young men to do their duty, but let them do it voluntarily and thereby develop their characters." ~ *Lee's common observation in his associations with his own sons, soldiers, and students.*

———————

"Young men must not expect to escape contact with evil, but must learn not to be contaminated by it." ~ *Lee while Superintendent of West Point.*

———————

"You must study to be frank with the world: frankness is the child of honesty and courage." ~ *Lee to his son Custis when Custis was a cadet at West Point.*

———————

"Never do a wrong thing to make a friend or keep one; the man who requires you to do so is dearly purchased at a sacrifice." ~ *Lee to his son Custis at West Point.*

———————

"If you have any fault to find with any one, tell him, not others, of what you complain; there is no more dangerous experiment than that of undertaking to be one thing before a man's face and another behind his back." ~ *Lee to his son Custis at West Point.*

———————

General Lee was called upon to testify at Jefferson Davis' preliminary hearing for treason. The prosecuting attorney was baiting Lee in order to get him to exonerate himself and make it appear that Davis was the one primarily responsible for the war and its outcome. General Lee caught on to the lawyer's scheme and stated: "I am responsible for what I did; and I cannot now recall any important movement I made which I would not have made had I acted on my own responsibility." Gentlemen must be willing to take responsibility for their failures, as well as their successes—regardless of the potential costs.

———

"As for myself, you young fellows might go to bushwhacking, but the only dignified course for me would be to go to General Grant and surrender myself and take the consequences of my acts." ~ *General Lee to General Alexander, 9 April 1865.*

———

"We should live so as to say and do nothing to the injury of any one. It is not only best as a matter of principle, but it is the path to peace and honor." ~ *Lee to his son Custis at West Point.*

———

"As long as I have any rations at all I shall divide them with my prisoners." ~ *General Lee on his treatment of Union prisoners. The good General was undoubtedly applying the words of the Saviour in Luke 6:35—"But love ye your enemies, and do good, and lend, hoping for nothing again; and your reward shall be great, and ye shall be the children of the Highest: for he is kind unto the unthankful and to the evil."*

———

"I am opposed to the theory of doing wrong that good may come of it. I hold to the belief that you must act right whatever the consequences." ~ *Lee to his son Custis.*

"Human virtue should be equal to human calamity." ~ *One of Lee's personal maxims.*

"We were duty bound to do our best, even if we perished in the endeavor." ~ *General Lee to General Pendleton.*

"I am of the opinion that all who can should vote for the most intelligent, honest, and conscientious men eligible to offices." ~ *General Lee to General Longstreet, 29 October 1867.*

"I think it is the duty of every citizen, in the present condition of the Country, to do all in his power to aid in the restoration of peace and harmony." ~ *General Lee in a letter to Judge Brockenbrough, 24 August 1865.*

"You must not feel anxious or unsettled, but persevere in your duty." ~ *Lee to his son Custis, 19 August 1859.*

"Efforts to do your duty will bring you a delight and gratification far surpassing all that idleness and selfishness can give." ~ *Lee to his son Custis, 4 May 1851.*

"We had, I was satisfied, sacred principles and rights to defend for which we were duty bound to do our best, even if we perished in the endeavor." ~ *General Lee on why he fought for the South.*

"We must be content with the bare necessities of life, if we can maintain clean hands and clear consciences." ~ *General Lee to General Butler.*

"Prepare the road for promotion and future advancement." ~ *Lee to his son, Fitzhugh, 30 May 1858.*

"Show your ability and worthiness of distinction." ~ *Lee to his son, Fitzhugh, 30 May 1858.*

"Hold yourself above every mean action. Be strictly honorable in every act, and be not ashamed to do right. Acknowledge right to be your aim and strive to reach it." ~ *Lee to his son, Custis, 4 May 1851.*

"I am unwilling to do what is wrong." ~ *Lee to his son, Custis, 14 December 1860.*

"Pay all debts as soon as possible." ~ *Lee to his son, Custis, 14 December 1860.*

"Bear manfully misfortunes and all will come right in the end." ~ *General Lee to Jefferson Davis, 5 August 1863.*

"Occupy yourself in aiding those more helpless than yourself." ~ *General Lee to one of his daughters, Christmas Day, 1861.*

"Take great care of your kind mother." ~ *Lee to his sons, 31 March 1846.*

"The real honest man is honest from conviction of what is right, not from policy." ~ *One of Lee's personal maxims.*

[1] These were the words of John Janney, President of the Virginia Secession Convention welcoming Lee into the old House of Delegates at the Capitol in Richmond on 25 April 1861.

[2] James Mackay, *William Wallace—Braveheart.* Mainstream Publishing, Edinburgh, Scotland, 1995, 267.

[3] Sir Walter Scott, *From Bannockburn to Flodden.* (Reprint) Cumberland House, Nashville, 2001, 63.

[4] Randolph H. McKim, *The Soul of Lee.* Longmans, Green and Co. London, 1917, 3.

[5] Philip A. Bruce, *Brave Deeds of Confederate Soldiers.* Originally published in 1916, (Reprint) Virginia Gentleman Books, Stuarts Draft, VA, 1999, 18.

[6] Thomas Jefferson in a letter to William Stephens Smith.

[7] Douglas Southall Freeman, *R.E. Lee.* New York: Charles Scribner's Sons, 1934, 1936, Volume I, 438.

[8] Freeman, Volume I, 438.

[9] Readers should carefully reflect on the fact that Virginia had been a political entity for more than two hundred years, and that Lee's roots in Virginia could be traced to the year 1640. The United States had only been a reality for about 80 years.

[10] Rev. J. William Jones, D.D. *Life and Letters of Robert Edward Lee.* Originally published in 1906 (Reprint) Harrisonburg, VA: Sprinkle Publications, 1986, 126.

[11] Bruce, 15.

[12] Rose Moritmer Ellzey MacDonald, *Mrs. Robert E. Lee.* Originally published in 1939. (Reprint) American Foundation Publications, Stuarts Draft, Virginia, 1998, 145.

[13] J.G. de Roulhac Hamilton, *The Life of Robert E. Lee for Young Gentlemen.* Originally published in 1917 under the title, *The Life of Robert E. Lee for Boys and Girls.* (Reprint) Virginia Gentleman Books, Stuarts Draft, VA, 2001, 95-96.

[14] Freeman, Volume I, page 431.

[15] Lee in a letter to son Custis Lee, 30 January 1861. See Douglas Southall Freeman's biography, Volume I, 420-421.

[16] Lee in a letter to Wade Hampton. See Freeman, Vol. I, 447.

[17] Freeman, Vol. IV, 490.

[18] Hamilton, 141.

Photos

*Front view of Lee Chapel on the campus of Washington
and Lee University in Lexington, Virginia.*

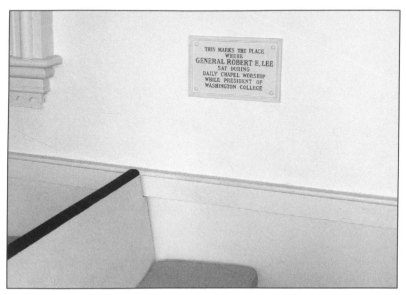

*This is the pew General Lee occupied during
worship services at Lee Chapel.*

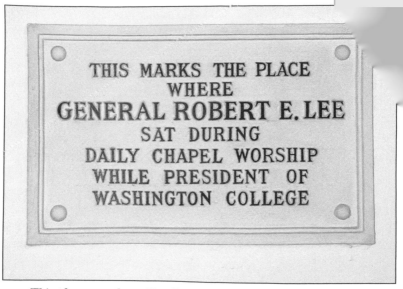

This plaque on the wall at Lee Chapel marks his pew and commemorates Lee's faithfulness in attending worship services.

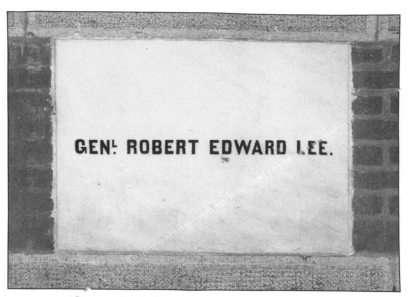

The spot that holds the mortal remains of General Lee—his crypt in the basement museum of Lee Chapel.

The tomb of General Lee's horse, Traveller, buried just outside the rear entrance to Lee Chapel's museum. Traveller's remains were moved to this location in 1971 by the United Daughters of the Confederacy.

Lee's home while he lived in Lexington. It is also the home in which he died and it is located just a few steps from the University, Lee Chapel, and the Episcopal church where Lee worshipped.

OUR

CHILDREN IN HEAVEN.

BY

WM. H. HOLCOMBE, M.D.

PHILADELPHIA

J. B. LIPPINCOTT & CO.

1868.

This is the title page to Our Children in Heaven, *published in 1868. It is likely the last book General Lee read before he died. His copy remains in his office to this day in the basement of Lee Chapel.*

Pencil sketch of General Lee done by the author's father at age twelve.

CHAPTER 5

Creation

━━◆◆━━

"Remember now thy Creator in the days of thy youth."

Ecclesiastes 12:1

"Have patience with Traveller, he was made nervous by the bursting of bombs around him during the war."

General Lee

General Lee was awed by Creation and God's handiwork. He often expressed the joy and peace that he experienced when he and his faithful horse, Traveller, would ride through beautiful Goshen Pass near Lexington, Virginia after the war. His love of Creation and of animals as God's creatures, as well as his concern for their well being, was well known. Lee was particularly fond of horses and cats. Solomon admonished us to treat animals with kind regard:

"A righteous man regardeth the life of his beast: but the tender mercies of the wicked are cruel." ~ Proverbs 12:10. Lee often regarded "the life of his beast":

"Many times I have seen General Lee manifest affection for Traveller, and Traveller always seemed to appreciate it. I have seen General Lee stand and gaze at the faithful old animal, apparently recalling scenes of the war. Then he would stroke Traveller's nose and hand him a lump of sugar. Traveller was his pet. A comrade and I frequently walked the road leading towards the Peaks of Otter. We often saw General Lee riding on the same road alone."[1]

———

Another incident that portrays the General's almost spiritual concern for animals is related by Rev. Randolph H. McKim in his biography of Lee:

"Near Richmond, in 1864, he and a group of soldiers attracted the fire of the enemy; whereupon Lee ordered the men back, but remained himself on the spot and then retired leisurely, but was observed to stop and pick up something. As if unconscious of danger to himself, Gen. Lee walked across the yard, picked up some small object from the ground, and placed it upon the limb of a tree above his head. He had risked his life for an unfledged sparrow that had fallen from its nest."[2]

Perhaps Lee thought of his Heavenly Father's concern for even the smallest of creatures as revealed in Matthew 10:29 ~ "Are not two sparrows sold for a farthing? and one of them shall not fall on the ground without your Father." Gentlemen should always take great effort in defending the weak and helpless.

———

The thoughtfulness of Lee regarding Creation and some of its weaker inhabitants was also shown by a comment Lee made to a Lexington neighbor who mentioned the beauty that a nearby forest fire added to a winter's night. In replying Lee stated: "It is beautiful but I have been thinking of the poor animals which must perish in the flames."[3]

———

"I enjoyed the mountains as I rode along. The views are magnificent—the valleys so beautiful, the scenery so peaceful. What a glorious world Almighty God has given us. How thankless and ungrateful we are." ~ *General Lee to his wife describing an area known as Buffalo Gap, Virginia, 4 August 1861.*

———

"What a beautiful world God in His loving kindness to His creatures has given us! What a shame that men endowed with reason and knowledge of right should mar his gifts!" ~ *General Lee to his wife in June of 1863.*

———

"Our good cow will be a loss to us, but her troubles are all over now, and I am grateful to her for what she had done for us. I hope that we did our duty to her." ~ *Lee commenting on the death of the family milk cow.*

———

"Tom, surnamed The Ripper, from the manner which he slaughters our enemies the rats and mice, is admired for his gravity and sobriety, as well as his strict attention to the pursuits of his race." ~ *General Lee writing to his daughter of his admiration for one of the family cats.*

———

"I still look with delight upon the mountains of my native State." ~ *General Lee to Captain M.F. Maury, 8 September 1865.*

———

"I do fell sorry for the poor creatures I see here, starved and driven from their homes for no reason whatsoever." ~ *General Lee commenting on conditions in war-torn Virginia.*

"Don't whip him, Captain, don't whip him. I have just such another foolish beast myself and whipping doesn't do any good." ~ *General Lee's admonition to an officer at Gettysburg.*

"I would like to go to some quiet place in the country and rest." ~ *General Lee to Sculptor Edward V. Valentine.*

"My daily walks are along, up and down the banks of the river, and my pleasure is derived from my own thoughts, and from the sight of the flowers and animals I there meet with." ~ *Lee in a letter to his family in December of 1856.*

"Always take care of the poor horses." ~ *General Lee to one of the Washington College professors.*

"I felt so elated when I found myself in the ancient Dominion that I nodded to all the trees I passed." ~ *General Lee on his return to Virginia in 1840.*

"The horse-chestnuts you mention in the garden were planted by my mother. You do not mention the spring, one of the objects of my earliest recollections. How my heart goes back to those early days." ~ *General Lee in a letter written to one of his daughters in 1861.*

"In the woods I feel sympathy with the trees and birds, in whose company I take delight." ~ *Lee to his wife, 5 June 1839.*

———◆———

"Existing orders require that all work on Sunday to cease, except those of necessity, in order that man and beast have one day to rest." ~ *General Lee in a letter to General Anderson, expressing his respect for the Sabbath and his concern for God's creatures.*

———◆———

"As far as possible imitate Nature." ~ *General Lee to Edward C. Gordon.*

———◆———

"My only pleasure is in my solitary evening rides which give me abundant opportunity for quiet thought." ~ *General Lee to his daughter-in-law.*

———◆———

"I purchased him in the mountains of Virginia in the autumn of 1861, and he has been my patient follower ever since . . . he passed through the fire . . . You must know what a comfort he is to me in my present retirement." ~ *Lee commenting on his horse, Traveller. General Lee and Traveller enjoyed a special relationship and were lovingly devoted to each other. A well-known Virginia school teacher in Lee's day, Captain Gordon McCabe, once noted that whenever Lee was riding Traveller, the horse, "always stepped as if conscious that he bore a king upon his back."*

———◆———

This special relationship that General Lee enjoyed with Traveller is further illustrated by the following story recounted by one of Lee's daughters. It also illustrates one aspect of Lee's superb horsemanship:

"One afternoon in July the General rode down to the canal-boat landing to put on board a young lady who had been visiting his daughters and was returning home. He dismounted, tied Traveller to a post, and was standing on the boat making his adieux, when some one called out that Traveller was loose. Sure enough, the gallant gray was making his way up the road, increasing his speed as a number of boys and men tried to stop him. My father immediately stepped ashore, called to the crowd to stand still, and advancing a few steps gave a peculiar low whistle. At the first sound, Traveller stopped and pricked up his ears. The General whistled a second time, and the horse with a glad whinny turned and trotted quietly back to his master, who patted and coaxed him before tying him up again. To a bystander expressing surprise at the creature's docility the General observed that he did not see how any man could ride a horse for any length of time without a perfect understanding being established between them." [4]

"Traveler is my only companion; I may also say my only pleasure. He and I, whenever practicable, wander out in the mountains and enjoy sweet confidence." ~ *General Lee commenting on his faithful steed.*

"Fine proportions, muscular figure, deep chest and short back, strong haunches...quick eye, small feet, and black mane and tail. Such a picture would inspire a poet, whose genius could then depict his worth and describe his endurance of toil, hunger, thirst, heat, cold, and the dangers and sufferings through which he passed." ~ *General Lee's summation of Traveller, for which he paid $200 in gold.*

"Above all things, learn at once to worship your Creator and to do His will as revealed in His Holy Book." ~ *Lee to his son, Robert, Jr.*

One last anecdote is worth mentioning and once again reveals Lee's concern for God's creatures. During the war, Lee observed a child whipping some mules to speed them up and admonished her, "Don't do that, my little child." A few moments later, the girl's memory failed her and she again struck the mules. Lee again admonished the young girl, in a more severe tone: "Anne, you must not do that again. My conscience is not entirely at ease about using these animals for this extra service, for they are half fed, as we all are."[5]

[1] Franklin L. Riley, *General Robert E. Lee After Appomattox*. The MacMillan Company, New York, 1930, 136.

[2] Randolph H. McKim, *The Soul of Lee*. Longmans, Green & Co., New York, 1918, 123.

[3] Douglas Southall Freeman, *R.E. Lee—Volume IV*. New York, Charles Scribner's Sons, 1935, 1936, 310.

[4] Riley, 93.

[5] Freeman, Volume III, 526.

CHAPTER 6

Wisdom

"Knowledge is proud that he has learned so much;
Wisdom is humble that he knows no more."

William Cowper

"A wise man will hear, and will increase learning;
and a man of understanding shall attain unto wise counsels."

Proverbs 5:1

General Lee's wisdom in handling difficult men and situations was legendary. He had such a command of his own will and passions that he was able to size up predicaments and adversaries with a detachment of self that enabled him to make decisions based on fact and likely outcome, rather than emotions or concern for his own welfare. He heeded well the warning embodied in Proverbs 25:28—"He that hath no rule over his own spirit is like a city that is broken down, and without walls." This was the secret of Lee's wisdom—self-control.

"Mildness and forbearance, tempered by firmness and judgment, will strengthen affection." ~ *Lee advice to his wife on the subject of child training.*

"Misfortune nobly borne, is good fortune." ~ *General Lee to sculptor Edward Valentine. This was one of Lee's favorite personal maxims and a quotation from* The Meditations of Marcus Aurelius.

"The better rule is to judge our adversaries from their standpoint, not from ours." ~ *One of Lee's personal maxims.*

"Get correct views of life, and learn to see the world in its true light. It will enable you to live pleasantly, to do good, and, when summoned away, to leave without regret." ~ *General Lee in a letter to his daughter, Mildred.*

"In this enlightened age there are few, I believe, but will acknowledge that slavery, as an institution, is a moral and political evil in any country." ~ *Lee in a letter to Mrs. Lee, 27 December 1856.*

"Their [slaves] emancipation will sooner result from the mild and melting influence of Christianity, than the storms of fiery Controversy. This influence though slow, is sure." ~ *Lee's thoughts on slavery.*

"I hope you are becoming more and more interested in making those around you happy, this is the true way to secure your own happiness." ~ *Lee to "Tabb," son Rooney's (Fitzgugh) second wife.*

"Do not worry yourself about things you cannot help, but

be content to do what you can for the well-being of what belongs properly to you." ~ *Lee to his wife, 7 January 1857.*

"The dominant party cannot reign forever, and truth and justice will at last prevail." ~ *General Lee to one of his sons, 26 February 1867.*

"By . . . encouraging our citizens to engage in the duties of life with all their heart and mind, with a determination not to be turned aside by thoughts of the past and fears of the future, our country will not only be restored in material prosperity, but will be advanced in science, in virtue, and in religion." ~ *General Lee to a magazine editor on his hope for the South.*

"Refrain from going where you have been prohibited, or have not the permission of your parents or teachers." ~ *Lee to his sons, 30 November 1845.*

"I deem it wisest for me to remain silent." ~ *General Lee after the war. Perhaps the General was heeding the counsel of King Solomon in Proverbs 10:19: "...he that refraineth his lips is wise."*

"Desire nothing too eagerly, nor think that all things can be perfectly accomplished according to our own notions." ~ *Lee to his wife, 7 January 1857.*

"If a gentleman can't understand the language of a gentleman, he must remain in ignorance, for a gentleman cannot write in any other way." ~ *General Lee to a Washington College professor.*

"Much of your future happiness will depend upon you." ~ *Lee in a letter to son Custis, 14 September 1851.*

"Meddle or interfere with nothing with which you have no concern." ~ *Lee to his sons, 30 November 1845. This is good advice for all gentlemen and, once again, the Book of Proverbs imparts the same counsel: "He that passeth by, and meddleth with strife belonging not to him, is like one that taketh a dog by the ears." Proverbs 26:17*

"Never marry unless you can do so into a family that will enable your children to feel proud of both sides of the house." ~ *General Lee to J.B. Hood.*

"Find time to read and improve your mind." ~ *Lee to his daughter, Mildred.*

"When a man makes a mistake, I call him to my tent, talk to him, and use the authority of my position to make him do the right things the next time." ~ *General Lee to General A.P. Hill.*

"Everyone is slandered, even the good." ~ *General Lee to his wife, 9 September 1861.*

"It is the living for whom I sorrow." ~ *General Lee to a bereaved father, 28 December 1862.*

"Those who oppose our purposes are not always to be regarded as our enemies." ~ *One of Lee's personal maxims.*

"Nothing will compensate us for the depression of the standard of our moral and intellectual culture." ~ *General Lee after the war.*

"The parent must bear constantly in mind, that to govern the child, he must show him that he can control himself." ~ *General Lee to J.B. Minor, 17 January 1867.*

"It is the part of wisdom to attend to your own affairs." ~ *Lee to his wife, 7 January 1857.*

"You must make friends while you are young, that you may enjoy them when old." ~ *Lee to son Custis, 13 March 1860.*

"It is easier to make our wishes conform to our means, than to make our means to conform to our wishes." ~ *Lee to one of his sons, 22 August 1860.*

"Never exceed your means. It will save you much anxiety and mortification, and enable you to maintain your independence of character and feeling." ~ *Lee to one of his sons, 22 August 1860.*

"One hour's sleep before midnight is worth two after that time." ~ *Lee on retiring early.*

———

"Do not appear to others what you are not." ~ *Lee to son Custis.*

———

"I hope you will always be distinguished for your avoidance of the 'universal balm,' whiskey, and every immorality." ~ *Lee to his son, Fitzhugh, 30 May 1858.*

———

"It is dangerous to meddle with. You have in store much better employment for your mouth." ~ *Lee to his son, "Rooney," about the use of tobacco, 1857.*

———

"You must use the resources you have so as to gain success." ~ *General Lee to General Jubal Early, 27 September 1864.*

———

"Listen to the teachings of your parents, obey their precepts, and from childhood to the grave pursue unswervingly the path of honor and of truth." ~ *General Lee in a letter to a young admirer, 29 May 1866.*

———

"Save all your money and invest it in some safe and lucrative way." ~ *Lee to his son, Custis, 17 March 1858.*

———

"Indiscriminate intimacies you will find annoying and entangling, and they can be avoided by politeness and civility." ~ *Lee to his son, "Rooney," 1857.*

"You must be aware of one thing, that those you deal with will consider their advantage and not yours. So while being fair and just, you must not neglect your interests." ~ *Lee's advice to his son, Custis.*

"I cannot consent to place in the control of others one who cannot control himself." ~ *General Lee on his refusal to promote certain officers due to their fondness of strong drink.*

"Some good is always mixed with the evil in this world." ~ *General Lee to one of his daughters, 11 June 1863.*

"Hold on to purity and virtue. They will sustain you in all trials and difficulties, and cheer you in every calamity." ~ *Lee to his son, "Rooney," 1 January 1859.*

"A man may manifest and communicate his joy, but he should conceal and smother his grief as much as possible." ~ *Lee to Mrs. Ann Fitzhugh.*

General Lee demonstrated his adherence to this maxim in a most poignant episode during the war. Lee was at his headquarters near Culpeper Court House in October of 1862. As was his usual custom, Lee read his morning mail quietly in his tent. Among the dispatches was a letter informing Lee of the death of his fourth child and dearly beloved daughter, Annie. His dearest Annie had contracted typhoid fever while staying at Jones Spring, North Carolina. She would forever be twenty-three. After reading the correspondence, Lee summoned Colonel Walter Taylor, his aide and adjutant general, and inquired if there were any pressing matters that needed to be attended to. Taylor then left Lee's tent to manage some routine tasks. A little while later, Taylor returned and entered Lee's tent unannounced. He was surprised to find General Lee weeping and, "overcome with grief, an open letter in his hands." Taylor would later write of the incident in his book, *Four Years with Lee:*

"His army demanded his first thought and care; to his men, to their needs, he must first attend, and then he could surrender himself to his private, personal affairs. Who can tell with what anguish of soul he endeavoured to control himself and to maintain a calm exterior, and who can estimate the immense effort necessary to still the heart filled to overflowing with tenderest emotions and to give attention to the important trusts committed to him, before permitting the more selfish meditation, grief, and prayer?"[1]

Taylor would also write, "General Lee was naturally of a positive temperament, and of strong passions; and it is a mistake to suppose him otherwise; but he held these in complete subjection to his will and conscience."[2]

———◆◆———

"That virtue is worth little that requires constant watching and removal from temptation." ~ *Lee to Martha ("Markie") Williams.*

———◆◆———

"There is scarcely anything that is right that we cannot hope to accomplish by labor and perseverance. But the first must be earnest and the second unremitting." ~ *Lee to Martha Williams.*

—◆—

"If you want to be missed by your friends, be useful." ~ *This phrase was oft' repeated by Lee to members of his family.*

—◆—

"I consider the character of no man affected by a want of success provided he has made an honest effort to succeed." ~ *Lee to the father of a West Point Cadet.*

[1] Rev. J. William Jones, D.D., *Life and Letters of Robert Edward Lee.* Originally published in 1906, (Reprint) Sprinkle Publications, Harrisonburg, VA, 1986, 197.

[2] John M. Taylor, *Duty Faithfully Performed*, Brassey's, Dulles, VA, 1999, 236.

CHAPTER 7

What Others Said
of Lee's Character

"Let another man praise thee."

Proverbs 27:2

"When a man's ways please the LORD, he maketh even his enemies to be at peace with him."

Proverbs 16:7

"So shalt thou find favour and good understanding in the sight of God and man."

Proverbs 3:4

The best confirmation of a man's quality of character is what others say about him. As Proverbs instructs us, those who please God will gain the respect and admiration of even their enemies. Robert E. Lee was, and is today, universally loved and respected. Even his enemies, during and after the war, had nothing but words of praise and admiration for him. The following comments by Lee's contemporaries and admirers demonstrate well the truth contained in Psalms 37:37—"Mark the perfect man, and behold the upright: for the end of that man is peace."

"Modest humility, simplicity, and gentleness, were most conspicuous in his daily life." ~ *J. William Jones.*

"When the future historian comes to survey the character of Lee, he will find it rising like a huge mountain above the undulating plain of humanity, and he will have to lift his eyes toward heaven to catch its summit." ~ *The Honorable Benjamin H. Hill of Georgia.*

"No people could live in the atmosphere of Lee and Jackson and not be the best." ~ *Booker T. Washington in a conversation with Virginia Congressman H. St. George Tucker.* [1]

"As he stood there, fresh and ruddy as a David from the sheepfold, in the prime of his manly beauty, and the embodiment of a line of heroic and patriotic fathers and worthy mothers, it was thus I first saw Robert E. Lee. I did not know then that he used no stimulants, was free from even the use of tobacco, and that he was absolutely stainless in his private life. I did not know then, as I do now, that he had been a model youth and young man; but I had before me the most manly and entire gentleman I ever saw." ~ *CSA Vice-President Alexander H. Stephens' first impression of Robert E. Lee.*

"He was always solicitous for the promotion of religion in the college, and warmly encouraged the work of the Young Men's Christian Association. He showed more emotion than on almost any other occasion in expressing his fervent wish that the students should all become sincere Christians." ~ *Rev. Randolph H. McKim.*

"His countrymen boldly challenge the world to produce from the annals of time another supreme soldier who was also such a supreme examplar of Christian virtue, of spotless manhood, of high chivalry, of unselfish devotion to duty, as the commander of the Army of Northern Virginia. Few among the great captains of history have surpassed or even equaled his achievements in the field of war; but is there one among them all that can compare with this hero of the Southern Confederacy in purity of life, in steadfast lifelong devotion to high ideal, in modest self-effacement, in freedom from selfish ambition, in sublime patience under adversity, in moderation in victory, in composure in defeat, in Christlike resignation?" ~ *Rev. Randolph H. McKim.*

"If I have ever come in contact with a sincere, devout Christian,—and one who, seeing himself to be a sinner, trusted alone in the merits of Christ,—who humbly tried to walk the path of duty, 'looking unto Jesus the author and finisher of our faith,' and whose piety was constantly exemplified in his daily life, that man was the world's great soldier, and model man, Robert Edward Lee." ~ *Rev. J. William Jones.*

"I tell you, sir, that Robert E. Lee is the greatest soldier now living, and if he ever gets the opportunity, he will prove himself the greatest captain of history." ~ *General Winfield Scott, just before the War Between the States.*

"He thought it to be the office of a college not merely to educate the intellect, but to make Christian men. The moral and religious character of the students was more precious in his eyes even than their intellectual progress, and was made the special object of his constant personal solicitude." ~ *Prof. Edward S. Joynes.*

"Self contained and serene, he acted as one who was conscious of having accomplished all that was possible in the line of duty, and who was undisturbed by the adverse conditions in which he found himself. There was no apparent excitement and no sign of apprehension as he issued his orders for the retreat of his sadly reduced army . . . It was a striking illustration of Christian fortitude, the result of an habitual endeavor to faithfully perform the duties of one's station, and of unquestioning trust in the decrees of an all-wise Creator." ~ *One of Lee's staff officers commenting on the somber retreat from Petersburg.*

"So great is my confidence in General Lee that I am willing to follow him blindfolded." ~ *Stonewall Jackson to Colonel Boteler.*

"I saw another sight in connection with Richmond's fall which I confess thrilled me a thousand times more than all the glory of the victorious armies of the Republic. It was a spectacle that broke upon me most unexpectedly; it came while the heavens were black with storm and the streets were wild with flooding rains. What I saw was a horseman. His steed was bespattered with mud, and his head was hung down as if worn by long traveling. The horseman himself sat his horse like a master; his face was ridged with self-respecting griefs; his garments were worn in the service and stained with travel; his hat was slouched and spattered with mud and only another unknown horseman rode with him, as if for company and for love. Even in the fleeting moment of his passing by my gate, I was awed by his incomparable dignity. His majestic composure, his rectitude and his sorrow, were so wrought and blended into his visage and so beautiful and impressive to my eyes that I fell into violent weeping. To me there was only one where this one was; there could be only one that day, and that one was still my own revered and cherished leader, stainless in honor, resplendent and immortal even in defeat, my own, my peerless chieftan, Robert E. Lee." ~ *Rev. W.E. Hatcher.*

"My own feelings, which had been quite jubilant on receipt of Lee's letter, were sad and depressed. I felt like anything rather than rejoicing at the downfall of a foe who had fought so long and so valiantly and had suffered so much for a cause." ~ *General Grant on Lee's surrender of the Army of Northern Virginia.*

"It may be said of Robert E. Lee that not only in the great crisis of his life was the spirit of renunciation supreme, but that all through his life, from the day when he publicly gave himself to the service of God in old Christ Church, Alexandria, he lived not to himself, but to God and to his fellow man." ~ *Rev. Randolph H. McKim.*

"I have made certain terms with Lee—the best and only terms. If I had told him and his army that their liberty would be invaded, that they would be open to arrest, trial and execution for treason, Lee would never have surrendered. I will resign the command of the army rather than execute any order directing me to arrest Lee or any of his commanders, so long as they obey the laws." ~ *General Grant upon learning of Lee's indictment for treason.*

"All the people except a few political leaders in the South will accept whatever he does as right and will be guided to a great extent by his example." ~ *General Grant.*

"I was at breakfast at the Spottswood Hotel when he entered the room, and was at once greatly...impressed by his appearance. [He had] strikingly handsome features, bright and penetrating eyes, his iron-gray hair closely cut, his face cleanly shaved except a mustache, he appeared every inch a soldier and a man born to command." ~ *Lee's staff member, Walter Taylor.*

"Lee is the greatest military genius in America." ~ *General Winfield Scott.*

"The world would never have known the full stature of General Lee's greatness if he had succeeded in his Titanic task of establishing the Southern Confederacy. It was in defeat, and trial, and toil, and reproach, that his greatness stood revealed in its true proportions." ~ *Rev. Randolph H. McKim.*

"Those virtues which were so admired by the public were all the more conspicuous in the home circle, and his private character was as stainless as it was unassailed by the breath of slander." ~ *Rev. J. William Jones.*

"I turned about, and there behind me, riding between my two lines, appeared a commanding form, superbly mounted, richly accoutered, of imposing bearing, noble countenance, with expression of deep sadness overmastered by deeper strength. It is none other than Robert E. Lee! ... I sat immovable, with a certain awe and admiration." ~ *Union General Joshua Chamberlain at Appomattox.*

"There is no recorded instance when his conversations in the field or barracks could not have been equally acceptable in a lady's drawing room. An examination of the two thousand letters which still exist fails to uncover the slightest suggestion of vulgarity." ~ *Bishop Robert R. Brown.*

"Probably no mortal man has passed through life, walking habitually nearer to his God, in thought, conversation, worship, sublime simplicity of faith, in action, whose watchword was duty; and devout contemplation, soothed by the spirit and promises of the Redeeming Christ!" ~ *Paul H. Hayne.*

"Robert Lee was one of the small company of great men in whom there is no inconsistency to be explained, no enigma to be solved. What he seemed, he was. He was—a wholly human gentleman, the essential elements of whose positive character were two and only two, simplicity and spirituality." ~ *Douglas Southall Freeman.*

"No youth or man so united the qualities that win warm friendship and command high respect [as did Lee]. For he was full of sympathy and kindness, genial and fond of gay conversation, and even of fun, while his correctness of demeanor and attention to all duties...gave him a superiority that every one acknowledged in his heart." ~ *Joseph E. Johnston.*

"Had his life been epitomized in one sentence of the Book he read so often, it would have been in the words, 'If any man will come after me, let him deny himself, and take up his cross daily, and follow me.'" ~ *Douglas Southall Freeman.*

"There was one place where General Lee could always be seen and that was at the daily prayer service in the college chapel." ~ *Professor C.A. Graves, University of Virginia.*

"His utterances were accepted as holy writ. No other earthly power could have produced such prompt acceptance of the final and irreversible judgment." ~ *Gamaliel Bradford.*

"If ever man made his life a true poem it was Lee." ~ *Gamaliel Bradford.*

"Lee had one intimate friend—God." ~ *Gamaliel Bradford.*

"It is an advantage to have a subject like Lee that one cannot help loving . . . I have loved him, and I may say that his influence upon my own life, thought I came to him late, has been as deep and as inspiring as any I have ever known." ~ *Gamaliel Bradford.*

"The fatherlands of Sidney and Bayard never produced a nobler soldier, gentleman, and Christian than Gen. Robert E. Lee." ~ *The London Standard.*

"No one, certainly, since the time of Napoleon has conquered against such immense odds." ~ *The London Times.*

"In strategy mighty, in battle terrible, in adversity as in prosperity a hero indeed, with the simple devotion to duty and the rare purity of the ideal Christian knight, he joined all the kingly qualities of a leader of men." ~ *Colonel Charles Cornwallis Chesney.*

"Like Napoleon, Lee's troops soon learned to believe him equal to every emergency that war would bring . . . Like Caesar he mixed with the crowd of soldiers freely, and never feared his position would be forgotten." ~ *Colonel Charles Cornwallis Chesney.*

"In the annals of the Lees for three centuries there was only one marital scandal and, so far as I know, not one divorce. For six generations after the emergence of the Lee family in America there were not more than two or three instances where it could be said that the Lees married persons who were not of equal blood and station with themselves. The result was the steady maintenance of the physical stamina and intellectual vigor of the stock for generations until its perfect flowering in one of the greatest human beings of modern times, Robert E. Lee." ~ *Douglas Southall Freeman.*

"He was the only one of all the men I have known who could laugh at the faults and follies of his friends in such a manner as to make them ashamed without touching their affections." ~ *Joseph E. Johnston.*

"He was a most exemplary student in every respect. He was never behind-time in his studies; never failed in a single recitation; was perfectly observant of the rules and regulations of the institution; was gentle, manly, unobtrusive, and respectful in all his deportment to teachers and his fellow students. His specialty was finishing up. He imparted a finish and a neatness to everything he undertook." ~ *Benjamin Hallowell ~ Young Lee's Quaker teacher in Alexandria, Virginia.*

"I always knew it was impossible to disobey my father." ~ *Robert E. Lee, Jr. writing of his father.*

"He was one who, though famous, was not honeycombed with ambition or tainted with cunning or cant, and though a soldier and wearing soldier's laurels, yet never craved or sought honors except as they bloomed on deeds done for the glory of his lawfully constituted authority; in short a soldier to whom the sense of duty was a gospel and a man of the world whose only rule in life was that life should be upright and stainless. I cannot but think Providence meant, through him, to prolong the ideal of the gentleman in the world . . . It is easy to see why Lee has become the embodiment of one of the world's ideals, that of the soldier, the Christian, and the gentleman. And from the bottom of my heart I thank Heaven . . . for the comfort of having a character like Lee's to look at." ~ *Union General Morris Schaff referring to Lee's surrender at which Schaff was present.*

—◦•◦—

"All the roads of life were carefully marked out for us by him." ~ *One of Lee's sons commenting on his father's guidance.*

—◦•◦—

"My contention is that Lee and the Army of Northern Virginia never sustained defeat. Finally, it is true, succumbing to exhaustion, to the end, they were not overthrown in fight." ~ *Charles Francis Adams.*

—◦•◦—

"Lee stands out as one of the greatest soldier of all times . . . undoubtedly one of the greatest if not the greatest who ever spoke the English tongue." ~ *Colonel Henderson, an English military critic.*

—◦•◦—

"He belonged to one branch of the church, and I to another. Yet in my intercourse with him—an intercourse rendered far more frequent and intimate by the tender sympathy he felt in my ill health—the thought never occurred to me that we belonged to different churches. His love for the truth, and for all that is good and useful, was such as to render his brotherly kindness and charity as boundless as were the wants and sorrows of the race." ~ *Stonewall Jackson's Pastor, Dr. W.S. White.*

—◦•◦—

"It is a notable thing that we see when we look back to men of this sort . . . In the midst of that crimson field stands this gentle figure,—a man whom you remember, not as a man who loved war, but as a man moved by all the high impulses of gentle kindness, a man whom men did not fear, but loved; a man in whom everybody who approached him marked singular gentleness, singular sweetness, singular modesty,—none of the pomp of the soldier, but all the simplicity of the gentleman. This man is in the center of that field, is the central figure of a great tragedy. A singular tragedy it seems which centers in a gentleman who loved his fellow men and sought to serve them by the power of love, and who yet, in serving them with the power of love, won the imperishable fame of a great soldier." ~ *President Woodrow Wilson on Robert E. Lee.*

———•·•———

"Intellectually he was cast in a gigantic mold. Naturally he was possessed of strong passions. He loved excitement, particularly the excitement of war. He loved grandeur. But all these appetites and powers were brought under the control of his judgment and made subservient to his Christian faith. This made him habitually unselfish and ever willing to sacrifice himself on the altar of duty and in the service of his fellows . . . He is an epistle, written of God and designed by God to teach the people of this country that earthly success is not the criterion of merit, nor the measure of greatness." ~ *Edward Clifton Gordon, Lee's aide at Washington College.*

———•·•———

"He was the ablest general, and to me, seemed the greatest man I ever conversed with . . . General Lee was one of the few men who ever seriously impressed and awed me with their natural inherent greatness. Forty years have come and gone since our meeting, yet the majesty of his manly bearing, the genial winning grace, the sweetness of his smile and the impressive dignity of his old-fashioned style of address, come back to me amongst the most cherished of my recollections

100

. . . His was indeed a beautiful character, and of him it might be written: "In righteousness he did judge and make war.'" ~ *Colonel Garnet Wolseley.*

"If willingness to sacrifice what is passionately prized next to honor itself is any criterion as to the degree of patriotism that begets such sacrifice, then the Southerners of whom Robert E. Lee is the type are to be counted among the patriots whose lives constitute the real riches of the nation." ~ *Editorial appearing in the* Outlook *upon the centennial of Lee's birth.*

"Never, was more beautifully displayed how a long and severe education of mind and character enables the soul to pass with equal step through this supreme ordeal; never did the habits and qualities of a lifetime, solemnly gathered into a few last hours, more grandly maintain themselves amid the gloom and shadow of approaching death. The recitence, the self-contained composure, the obedience to proper authority, the magnanimity and Christian meekness that marked all his actions, preserved their sway, in spite of the inroads of disease, and the creeping lethargy that weighed down his facilities. As the old hero lay in the darkened room, or with the lamp and hearth fire casting shadows upon his calm, noble front, all the massive grandeur of his form, and face, and brow remained; and death seemed to lose its terrors, and to borrow a grace and dignity in sublime keeping with the life that was ebbing away. The great mind sank to its last repose, almost with the equal poise of health." ~ *W.P Johnston, a professor at Washington and Lee and son of Lee's old comrade, Sidney Johnston, observing General Lee the night of October 10th, 1870.*

"On a quite autumn morning, in the land he loved so well, and, as he held, served so faithfully, the spirit of Robert Edward Lee left the clay which it had so much ennobled, and traveled out of this world into the great and mysterious land. The expressions of regret which sprang from the few who surrounded the bedside of the dying soldier, on yesterday, will be swelled today into one mighty voice of sorrow, resounding throughout our country, and extending over all parts of the world where his great genius and his many virtues are known. For not to the Southern people alone shall be limited the tribute of a tear over the dead Virginian. Here in the North, forgetting that the time was when the sword of Robert Edward Lee was drawn against us—forgetting and forgiving all the years of bloodshed and agony—we have claimed him as one of ourselves; have cherished and felt proud of his military genius as belonging to us; have recounted and recorded his triumphs as our own; have extolled his virtue as reflecting upon us—for Robert Edward Lee was an American, and the great nation which gave him birth would be today unworthy of such a son if she regarded him lightly.

Never had mother nobler son. In him the military genius of America developed to a greater extent than ever before. In him all that was pure and lofty in mind and purpose found lodgment. Dignified without presumption, affable without familiarity, he united all those charms of manner which made him the idol of his friends and of his soldiers, and won for him the respect and admiration of the world. Even as, in the days of his triumph, glory did not intoxicate, so, when the dark clouds swept over him, adversity did not depress. From the hour that he surrendered his sword at Appomattox to the fatal autumn morning, he passed among men, noble in the quiet, simple dignity, displaying neither

bitterness nor regret over the irrevocable past. He conquered us in misfortune by the grand manner in which he
sustained himself, even as he dazzled us by his genius when
the tramp of his soldiers resounded through the valleys of
Virginia. And for such a man we are all tears and sorrow
today. Standing beside his grave, all men of the South and
men of the North can mourn with all the bitterness of four
years of warfare erased by this common bereavement. May
this unity of grief—this unselfish manifestation over the loss
of the Bayard of America—in the season of dead leaves and
withered branches which this death ushers in, bloom and
blossom like the distant coming spring into the flowers of a
heartier accord." ~ *Editorial from the* New York Herald *the day
after Lee's death.*

"He was the only man I ever met who measured up to my
concept of Washington. The grandeur of his appearance is
beyond my power of portraiture. He is ineffable." ~ *James C.
Nisbet.*

"The beauty of God can be seen in his endless pursuit of
righteousness . . . In short, Lee's greatness lies in his response
to the initiative of a loving God and to the faith it supplied."
~ *Bishop Robert R. Brown.*

"In dedicating his future life to the holy work of educat-
ing the youth of his country, Gen. Lee presents a new and
interesting phase of his grand and heroic character—a character than which no more perfect model exists among living
men. 'Tis a solid fabric, and will well support the laurels that
adorn it.' Let the young men of this country, North as well

as South, be wise, and profit not less by his precepts than by his great example." ~ *Judge John Brockenbrough, Rector of Washington College, in an announcement of Lee becoming president of Washington College, 1 September 1865.*

———

[1] Henry Boley, *Lexington in Old Virginia.* Originally published in 1936, (Reprint) Liberty Hall Press, Washington & Lee University, Lexington, VA, 1974, 129.

CHAPTER 8

General Lee's Reading Habits

—————

"Amusement is the satisfaction of those who cannot think; entertainment is the gratification of those who cannot read."

Alexander Pope

"Reading feeds the brain. It is evident that most minds are starving to death."

Benjamin Franklin

"...give attendance to reading..."

Apostle Paul

R obert E. Lee was always concerned about the type of books his sons and daughters read—as all parents should be. On more than one occasion, he advised them to avoid frivolous reading material—advice his own father had imparted to young Robert. The appetite of today's youth for romance and mystery novels, and other vain writings, should grieve our hearts. Many of the classics are systematically being removed from the shelves of our Nation's libraries and being replaced with nonsensical tales of sorcery and shallow stories about pop culture figures—junk food for the brain, which in turn pollutes the soul. Many of today's youth would rather be entertained than enlightened and prefer amusement to ambition—enlightenment and ambition naturally encouraged and nurtured by being exposed to virtuous books.

The following essay (edited) was taken from one of the most cherished books in my library—*General Robert E. Lee After Appomattox.*[1] This book was published in 1930 and is a collection of essays by Lee's students, fellow Confederates, and other acquaintances. This fascinating chapter reveals Lee's tastes in reading material and proves he was a serious student of history, government, and the divine truths of God's Word. While Lee was a serious reader, he also read to comfort his wounded soul—a soul wounded not only by the South's suffering, but also by the unexpected death of his beloved daughter, Annie, in 1862.

The Bible and his prayer book were constant and well-worn companions. The Scriptures and prayers solaced his spirit while fortifying his faith in a brighter and happier hereafter. Lee read other theological works as well. General Lee was a subscriber to the "Southern Churchman" which was published by the Episcopal Church, of which he was a faithful member, and featured such articles as, "Conversion and Baptism," "The Second Coming of Christ," and "The Christian View of Death."[2]

It is very possible that the last book General Lee read before his fatal illness, was a book titled, *Our Children in Heaven* by William H. Holcombe.[3] This book, published in 1868, was dedicated "To those who have been bereaved of their children." Undoubtedly its words offered Lee comfort, as he sensed that he would soon be united with the daughter he adored in heaven. The book remains in Lee's office in the basement of Lee Chapel to this day. I have included the chapter on Lee's reading habits to serve as an example to aspiring young gentlemen to be judicious and deliberate in selecting their reading material.

What General Lee Read After the War

by Franklin L. Riley,
Washington and Lee University

General Lee read very few newspapers and made little effort to inform himself about the political storm that raged throughout the country after the war. With the exception of a single reference to the *Washington Star,* the *New York Times,* the *Watchman,* and a few casual references to other papers, not named, his letters never referred to current newspapers.

From these facts and many others which might be cited, one feels warranted in saying that General Lee spent no time after the war in the study of military strategy or in the serious study of any European wars of that day. These statements will not warrant one in concluding that General Lee was not interested in history. He made personal appeals to many former Confederate officers to record the histories of their campaigns. He advised his daughter Mildred, "Read history, works of truth, not novels and romances. Get correct views of life and learn to see the world in its true light," In one of his most sublime paragraphs, he said: "It is history that teaches us to hope. In a letter expressing a hope that Generals Beauregard and Johnston would write histories of their campaigns, he said: "Everyone should do all in their power to collect and disseminate the truth, in the hope that it may find a place in history and descend to posterity." His interest in a true history of the war was further shown by his criticism of a glaring inaccuracy, which, as he, "learned from others," had appeared in the works of "various authors of the 'Life of Jackson.' "

It is interesting to note that General Lee's literary ambitions were along the lines of history and biography. The first of these was the preparation of a complete history of the Army of Northern Virginia. Soon after the surrender at Appomattox he began collecting materials for such a work. In the summer of 1865 he sent a circular letter to many of his old officers asking for their assistance and cooperation, saying, "I am desirous that the bravery and devotion of the Army of Northern Virginia be transmitted to posterity. This is the only tribute that can be paid to the worth of its noble officers and soldiers." Dr. J. Wm. Jones makes the following valuable comment on this phase of General Lee's literary activity:

"Up to his fatal illness, General Lee was busily engaged in collecting material, and seemed very anxious to write a history of his campaigns; but his object was to vindicate *others rather than himself.* He said to one of his generals, in a letter asking for his official reports: 'I shall write this history, not to vindicate myself, or to promote my own reputation, I want that the world shall know what my poor boys, with their small numbers and scant resources, succeeded in accomplishing.' "

General Lee was more fortunate in his second literary ambition, which was the preparation of a biographical sketch of his father for a new edition of the life of Gen. Henry ("Light Horse Harry") Lee. It was published by the University Publishing Company under the title: "Memoirs of the War in the Southern Department of the United States, by Henry Lee...with Revisions and a Biography of the Author by Robert E. Lee." This work seems to have been finished June 1, 1869, less than eighteen months before General Lee's death. His numerous footnote references not only in the Biography but throughout the volume, the latter of which are designated by the abbreviation, "Ed.," indicate that his investigations were characterized by his usual patience and thoroughness.

In the winter of 1866, Mr. Worsley, an English admirer,

contributed a copy of his translation of the *Iliad* to the General's meager library. In acknowledging the receipt of the book, General Lee wrote:

"Its perusal has been my evening's recreation, and I have never enjoyed the beauty and grandeur of the poem more than as recited by you. The translation is as truthful as powerful, and faithfully reproduces the imagery and rhythm of the bold original. The undeserved compliment to myself in prose and verse on the first leaves of the volume, I receive as your tribute to the merit of my countrymen who struggled for constitutional government."

One of his sons, Capt. R.E. Lee, gives a delightful glimpse into his father's family circle shortly after the removal to Lexington: "That winter," says he, "my father was accustomed to read aloud in the long evenings to my mother and sisters, 'The Grand Old Bard,' equally to his own and listener's enjoyment."

General Lee must have derived much pleasure from reading also the *Thoughts of the Emperor Marcus Aurelius,* a copy of the second edition of which came from Professor George Long, another English admirer.

Mr. Valentine, the sculptor, treasured the following remark made by General Lee while in the artist's studio in Richmond, May, 1870: "Misfortune nobly borne is good fortune." This sentiment was so appropriate to the subject of their conversation that Mr. Valentine thought it was original with General Lee until sometime after his death. In after years this quotation was found in *Meditations of Marcus Aurelius.* General Lee was so averse to every appearance of pedantry that he used this noble sentiment without giving the source from which it came.

Captain Lee gives us a further glimpse into his father's family circle by the statement that General Lee would often read to his invalid wife in the evenings.

General Lee's private library after the war was very small, since the books left at Arlington had been scattered during hostilities. The meager salary, from which he supported his family and made liberal contributions to religious and charitable objects, evidently afforded little means for the purchase of new books for his own private library, though he bought "a collection of suitable books" for the library of the newly organized Y.M.C.A. of the college and the more important library of the Franklin Society. Records show that General Lee made constant use of both of these libraries.

The first library book he used after his removal to Lexington was Goldsmith's *Rome.* It was read about the time, probably immediately after, he had finished reading Worsley's *Iliad,* referred to above. An examination of this book will suggest reasons why it appealed to General Lee. Chapter I treats of the rise of Julius Caesar and the overthrow of the Roman Republic. Chapter II treats of the period of anarchy which followed Caesar's death and the final settlement of the constitution and the organization of the Empire under Augustus. Chapters III and IV contain many suggestive passages which would have appealed to ex-Confederates in the late 1860's, when they had many reasons to fear wholesale confiscation, disenfranchisement and even the loss of life. He must have read and pondered many sentences like the following: "The most sacred rights of nature were violated; three hundred senators; and above two thousand knights were included in this terrible proscription; their fortunes were confiscated, and their murderers enriched with the spoil."

General Lee was reading this book when the clouds of Reconstruction had begun to appear above our political horizon. Was he studying the causes which led to the overthrow of the Roman Republic in an effort to see whether similar dangers were then threatening his own country? Was he trying to get light from ancient history on the possible courses of events in his own day? He could not then know, of course, that there was not another Augustus Caesar awaiting an opportunity to overthrow the liberties of this country. Perhaps he was testing his axiom, cited above: "It is history that teaches us to hope."

In April or May, 1866, he read the writings of Rev. Alex. B. Grosart, which he had received from the author, in Liverpool, England. The second library book he used was the *Memoirs of the Duchess D'Abrantes* (Madam Junot). Probably General Lee's interest in this book, came from his desire to write an account of his own campaigns. He may have examined it for the purpose of learning particularly of the campaigns of Napoleon as treated by the wife of one of Napoleon's generals. On the other hand, he may have been interested in the conditions which produced this modern despot, as the book treats of the rise of Napoleon and the events leading to the establishment of his Empire. I do not think that there are any sentiments in the work which would have appealed to a man of General Lee's character. We must note, however, that this was the beginning of a study of biography which extended through a period of almost a year and a half.

The third book, in chronological order, charged to General Lee on the library records, was Spark's *Washington* (volume omitted).

While he was devoting his brief and irregular periods of leisure to the study of history, his wife and daughters at Rockbridge Baths, eleven miles distant, were doubtless reading the three books which followed on the record: *Bleak House,* and *Leo the Tenth,* Vols. III and IV. Shortly after Mrs. Lee's return home a volume of Hood's *Works* was also taken out of the library.

In December, 1866, he took out Marshall's *Washington,*

Vols. III, IV and V, and Spark's *Washington,* Vol. X, and *American Constitution* (edition not given). These books were all returned December 27 and 30. This must have been the period of General Lee's most intense literary activity while in Lexington. It is worth recording that in this period he wrote a very notable letter to Lord Acton.

With the beginning of the new year (1867) he must have been busy with college duties, as the library record shows that he did not resume his literary work until February 19. He then took out of the library Walburn's *Biographical Dictionary* and a *Gazetteer of the United States* (edition not given). March 14, he turned his attention to Ramsey's *American Revolution,* Vols. I and II, and later (March 30) to Henning's *Statutes.* About this time he wrote that he had received "from Fitz Lee a narrative of the operations of his division of cavalry," and asked his son, General W.H.F. Lee, for a full report of his war operations. These glimpses give us the picture of a busy college executive utilizing his small fragments of spare time at work on his twofold literary task.

April 3, 1867, he found diversion in a copy of *Calculus,* his first choice of books from the college library. Three weeks later he procured from the same source a copy of Webster's *Unabridged Dictionary.*

In July and August of that year he was at White Sulphur and Old Sweet Springs with his family, primarily for his wife's health. At the latter place he was taken ill. This prevented his return to Lexington until the middle of September, just before the opening of the session. He wrote to one of his sons (September 20): "I am still so feeble that I cannot attend to the business of the college." A month later (October 25) he wrote: "I have been quite sick but am better now." Yet, a fortnight before this latter date he had returned to his literary task, using Marshall's *Life of Washington,* Vols. III, IV and V. With the return of these three volumes (November 14) I find no evidence from the library record of any further serious study on his part, though he did not send the "Biography" of his father and the notes to the volume he was editing to the press until June 1, 1869, judging by the date of the Preface.

The Christmas season of 1867 found only two library books in his home. These were Goldsmith's *Vicar of Wakefield* and Bunyan's *Pilgrim's Progress*. What appropriate selections for Christmas reading! One wonders whether the General still read aloud to his family "in the long evenings" of that winter, as he had done in other years.

As intimated above, there was a marked change in the character of his reading after 1867. From that date he used no more library books on American history or biography. Poetry, choice fiction, current magazines and European history fill the remainder of the library record. Did he regard his recent sickness as an evidence of failing strength and a warning that his literary activity must cease? Possibly so, though Captain Lee felt sure that by the latter part of January his father "had fully recovered." It is more probable that this change from his own unfinished task was prompted by the literary tastes of his invalid wife, who as he said, suffered that winter and spring "more than usual . . . from her rheumatic pains." His son, Captain Lee, tells us: "He sat with her daily, entertaining her with accounts of what was doing in the college, and the news of the village, and would often read to her in the evenings."

The college library contributed, January 7, 1868, two large illustrated volumes of *Favorite English Poems* to the entertainment of the household. These books are "illustrated with 300 engravings on wood." Volume I contains a collection of choice poems from Chaucer to Pope, Volume II, from "Thompson to Tennyson." That they were read with interest is indicated by the fact that they were renewed

January 24 and were kept out until February 11. *Robinson Crusoe* then came in for a six days' reading, perhaps by General Lee's little niece, who was a member of his household that session.

About this time, he received from the library a two-volume edition of the *Life of Goethe* to be followed, two days later, by a copy of *Faust*. All of these were returned May 4. He then read, with much interest, I am sure, the first volume of Dr. Kane's *Arctic Expedition*. Probably the author, was a personal acquaintance. The last library book used that spring was a volume of Shakespeare's *Works*.

In the summer of 1868, he made another effort to find recreation and restoration of health for his invalid wife at some of the many celebrated health resorts near Lexington. Additional cares also came with the sickness of his daughter, Mildred, who had typhoid fever while at Warm Springs. He nursed her back to health in time to return to Lexington for the opening of the session of 1868-69.

Then followed a period of over six months in which he read nothing from the library, except current magazines. A book entitled *Queens of the Country* follows on the record (March 7, 1869). It was probably Mrs. Jameson's *Memoirs of Celebrated Female Sovereigns*. This volume may have been chosen for its sketch of Queen Anne, in order to link together the periods of English history which had already received attention.

The remainder of the spring of 1869 was devoted to various volumes on French history. In November General Lee contracted a severe cold, which was the beginning of the attack that was to prove fatal. In December he wrote that he was better, adding, "The Doctors still have me in hand, but I fear can do no good." In fact, he seemed to realize from the beginning that this attack was mortal.

Under these circumstances, one would not expect to find

evidence of extensive reading. Yet on November 20 two issues of *Blackwood's Magazine* were brought to his sick room. One issue of January, 1860, contained an article on "Rambles at Random in the Southern States," which gives the observations of an English traveler of keen though sympathetic mind, who had spent some time in the South before the war.

Here the library record closes. It reveals the fact that his library reading, during his five years in Lexington, which had carried him into many countries and into different periods of history and literature ended with a delightful article on his own beloved Southland.

This sketch would fall short of a true representation of what General Lee read after the war, if it should omit his two favorite books, which he always kept in his small private library, and which were in constant use. These were the Episcopal prayer book and the Bible. His appreciation of his prayer book is shown by his desire to supply copies to the soldiers who wished for them, and his present of a dozen copies,—all he had, save one, to as many soldiers. One of his sons says that "family prayers . . . were read every morning just before breakfast," which was served at seven o'clock, and another son warned his wife that "to please his father, she must be always ready for family prayers." His daughter-in-law said that "she did not believe that General Lee would have an entirely high opinion on any person, even General Washington, if he could return to earth, if he were not ready for prayers!"

But the greatest of all books in his estimation was the Bible. Upon appropriate occasions, he quoted its precepts, but never in the spirit of cant. In reproof of a minister who had said harsh things about the North in connection with General Lee's indictment for treason, he said: "Doctor, there is a good book, which I read and you preach from, which says: 'Love your enemies, bless them that curse you, do good to them that hate you and pray for them that despitefully use you.'"

During the war, "even amid his most active campaigns, he found time to read every day some portion of God's Word." The habit, followed so tenaciously on the field, was never given up in the quietude of the home; for he could then have his regular seasons for this delightful exercise. His appreciation of the Bible was shown by his interest in the Rockbridge County Bible Society, of which he was president from the time of its reorganization after the war (1868) until his death. In his letter, accepting the position, he spoke of his desire to help extend "the inestimable knowledge of the priceless truths of the Bible." In acknowledging the receipt of a Bible from some English admirers he referred to it as "a book in comparison with which all others in my eyes are of minor importance, and which all my perplexities and distresses had never failed to give me light and strength." In a letter acknowledging the receipt of a beautiful Bible for use in the college chapel he said, "it is a book which supplies the place of all others, and one that cannot be replaced by any other." The day after his death Dr. J. William Jones noticed on the table "a well-used pocket Bible, in which was written . . . 'R. E. Lee, Lieutenant-colonel, U.S. Army.' He says: "As I turned its leaves and saw how he had marked many passages, especially those teaching the great doctrines of Salvation by Grace, Justification by Faith, or those giving the more precious promises to the believer, I thought of how, with simple faith, he took this blessed Book as the man of his counsel and the light of his pathway; how its precious promises cheered him amid the afflictions and trials of his eventful life; and how its glorious hopes illuminated for him the 'valley and shadow of death.'"

[1] Franklin L. Riley, *General Robert E. Lee After Appomattox.* New York, The MacMillan Company, 1922.

[2] Bishop Robert R. Brown, *And One Was a Soldier—The Spiritual Pilgrimage of Robert E. Lee.* White Mane Books, Shippensburg, PA, 1998, 24.

[3] Brown, 24.

Epilogue

A s has been demonstrated by Lee's own words, as well as those who knew him, the life of Robert E. Lee is certainly one that young gentlemen can and should emulate. His many Christian virtues, marked by his conduct in war and peace, stand as a testament to the perfection that God desires for all those who name the name of Christ.

Virtue and honor are the inherent fruits borne of seeking the "wisdom of the ancients." American society, especially our youth crazed culture, seems to abhor any sentiment that it deems antiquated or old-fashioned. This is one of the fatal signs of a civilized society:

"Nearly four hundred years of America's hard earned accounts —the principles we established, the battles we fought, the morals we upheld for century after century, our very humility before God—now flow promiscuously through our hands like blood onto sand, squandered and laid waste by a generation...More than a pity, more than a shame, it is despicable."~ Mark Helprin. [1]

As we have become all knowing and self-sufficient in our own self-declared enlightenment, we have rejected the tried and proven values of our fathers—and the God of our fathers. We do so because we believe we are wiser and more reasonable. It is elitism at its worst. At the heart of this elitist mindset is pride; pride in one's self, one's knowledge, and one's own abilities—something that Lee would have disdained. Moderns fail to realize, or even worse, fail to acknowledge, that we stand on the shoulders of all who have gone before us. Without their wisdom, their successes and their failures, we would be much less than what we are. Richard Weaver so eloquently described this modern mindset with these words:

"They have lost a sense of the difficulty of things. Their institutionalized world is a product of toil and discipline: of this they are no longer aware. Like the children of rich parents, they have been pampered by the labor and self-denial of those who went before; they begin to think that luxuries, though unearned, are rightfully theirs." [2]

In failing to retain the eternal truths and "wisdom of the ancients" we suffer the unavoidable consequences revealed by the Apostle Paul in the first chapter of the book of Romans. We, "...do those things which are not convenient..."[3]

While making great technological strides, American society seems to have stepped backward in our virtues and our common courtesies. We have become a coarser, more selfish, and violent society seemingly at war with itself. In a word we have become *wicked,* and the Scriptures tell us that there is no peace for the wicked.[4]

This is in marked contrast to Lee's life. Though he fought in two wars and suffered the burden of the South's crushing defeat, he had an inner peace that comes through striving for perfection—the perfection of Christ:

"Mark the perfect man, and behold the upright: for the end of that man is peace." Psalms 37:37

Peace, wisdom and virtue—things that Robert E. Lee would wish for all young men reading this book; things that can be obtained by choosing duty and honor over convenience and conformity, and most importantly, by choosing to follow Christ, as General Lee did. His wish for his son is one I'm sure he'd wish for all the young men reading this book:

"May you have many happy years, all bringing you an increase of virtue and wisdom, all witnessing your prosperity in this life, all bringing you nearer everlasting happiness thereafter. May God in His great mercy grant me this my constant prayer."[5]

As readers of this volume consider the example of Robert E. Lee, may you never forget the source of his strength and may you prayerfully consider the words of Randolph McKim:

"Young men, do not disappoint the hope and the prayer of this revered and beloved hero! Complete his victory today by surrendering to the benignant sway of that divine Redeemer whom he loved so well!" ~ *Rev. Randolph H. McKim.*[6]

TIIE END

[1] Mark Helprin. *Statesmanship and its Betrayal,* Imprimis, April 1998, Volume 27, Number 4, Hillsdale College, Hillsdale, Michigan, 3.

[2] Richard Weaver, *The Southern Tradition at Bay.* Regnery Gateway, Washington, D.C., 1989, 17.

[3] Romans 1:28

[4] Isaiah 57:20

[5] Lee to his son in December of 1851.

[6] This quote is taken from a sermon titled *Lee the Christian Hero,* preached by Rev. Randolph H. McKim, D.D., LL.D, at

Lee Memorial Church in Lexington, Virginia on the occasion of General Lee's 100th birthday celebration, Sunday, 20 January 1907.

Bibliography

Bedwell, Randall. *May I Quote You, General Lee?* Nashville: Cumberland House, 1997.

Boley, Henry. *Lexington in Old Virginia.* Lexington, VA: Liberty Hall Press, Washington & Lee University, 1974. (Reprint—Originally published in 1936.)

Brown, Bishop Robert R. *And One Was a Soldier—The Spiritual Pilgrimage of Robert E. Lee.* Shippensburg, PA: White Mane Books, 1998.

Bradford, Gamaliel. *Lee the American.* Alexander, NC: Blue/Gray Books, 1998.

Bruce, Philip Alexander. *Brave Deeds of Confederate Soldiers.* Stuarts Draft, VA: Virginia Gentleman Books, 1999. (Reprint—Originally published in 1916.)

Cannon, Devereaux D., Jr. *The Wit and Wisdom of Robert E. Lee.* Gretna, LA: Pelican, 1997.

Crocker, H.W., III. *Robert E. Lee on Leadership—Executive*

Lessons in Character, Courage and Wisdom. Rocklin, CA: Forum/Prima Publishing, 1999.

Freeman, Douglas Southall. *R.E. Lee—Volumes I—IV.* New York: Charles Scribner's Sons, 1935, 1936.

Freeman, Douglas Southall. *Lee of Virginia.* New York: Charles Scribner's Sons, 1958.

Grant, George and Karen. *Lost Causes—The Romantic Attraction of Defeated Yet Unvanquished Men and Movements.* Nashville: Cumberland House, 1999.

Grant, George and Karen. *Shelf Life—How Books Have Changed the Destinies and Desires of Men and Nations.* Nashville: Cumberland House, 1999.

Hamilton, J.G. de Roulhac. *The Life of Robert E. Lee for Young Gentlemen.* Stuarts Draft, VA: Virginia Gentleman Books, 2001. (Reprint—Originally published in 1917 under the title, *The Life of Robert E. Lee for Boys and Girls.*)

Hatcher, William E., LL. D., L.H.D. *Along the Trail of the Friendly Years.* New York: Fleming H. Revell, 1910.

Helprin, Mark. *Statesmanship and its Betrayal.* Hillsdale, Michigan: Imprimis, April 1998, Volume 27, Number 4.

Jones, Rev. J. William, D.D. *Christ in the Camp.* Harrisonburg, VA: Sprinkle Publications, 1986. (Reprint—Originally published in 1887.)

Jones, Rev. J. William, D.D. *Life and Letters of Robert Edward E.*

Lee—Soldier and Man. Harrisonburg, VA: Sprinkle Publications, 1986. (Reprint—Originally published in 1906.)

Jones, Rev. J. William, D.D. *Personal Reminiscences of General Robert E. Lee.* New York: Tom Doherty Associates, LLC, 2003. (Reprint—Originally published in 1875.)

Long, A.L., *Memoirs of Robert E. Lee—His Military and Personal History.* Secaucus, N.J: The Blue and Grey Press, 1983. (Reprint -Originally published in 1886.)

MacDonald, Rose Moritmer Ellzey. *Mrs. Robert E. Lee.* Stuarts Draft, Virginia: American Foundation Publications, 1998. (Reprint—Originally published in 1939.)

Mackay, James. *William Wallace—Braveheart.* Edinburgh, Scotland: Mainstream Publishing, 1995.

McKim, Randolph H. *The Soul of Lee.* New York: Longmans, Green & Co., 1918.

Riley, Franklin L. *General Robert E. Lee after Appomattox.* New York: The MacMillan Company, 1930.

Robertson, James I. *Stonewall Jackson—The Man, The Soldier. The Legend.* New York: MacMillan Publishing, 1997.

Scott, Sir Walter. *From Bannockburn to Flodden.* Nashville: Cumberland House, 2001.

Taylor, John M. *Duty Faithfully Performed—Robert E. Lee and His Critics.* Dulles, VA: Brassey's, 1999.

Thomas, Andrew Peyton. *Crime and the Sacking of America— The Roots of Chaos.* Washington, D.C.: Brassey's, 1994.

Thomas, Emory M. *Robert E. Lee—A Biography.* New York: W.W. Norton & Company, 1995.

Weaver, Richard M. *The Southern Tradition at Bay—A History of Postbellum Thought.* Washington, D.C.: Regnery, 1989.

Whipple, Wayne. *The Heart of Lee.* Philadelphia: The John C. Winston Co., 1923.

Wilkins, J. Steven. *The Call of Duty—The Sterling Nobility of Robert E. Lee.* Nashville: Cumberland House, 1997.

About the Author

Richard G. Williams, Jr. is an insurance professional, publisher (Virginia Gentleman Books—VirginiaGentleman.com), and free-lance writer living with his wife and children in Virginia's Shenandoah Valley. He writes a regular column, "Business Lessons from History," for *Business Reform Magazine* (BusinessReform.com) and contributes to *Homeschooling Today Magazine* (HomeSchoolingToday.com). He is also a regular contributor to *The Chalcedon Report* (Chalcedon.edu). Williams is active in historical preservation as a member of the Stonewall Jackson Brigade Camp of the Sons of Confederate Veterans in Lexington, VA where he serves as the camp Chaplain. He helped produce the video series, "Institute on the Constitution," with constitutional attorney and law professor John Eidsmoe, which won a national award from the *Freedoms Foundation at Valley Forge*. Williams also served twelve years in Virginia government and as an appointee of former Virginia Governor, George Allen. Williams can be contacted at: contact@VirginiaGentleman.com.